DEVOTIONS FROM HERstory

31 DAYS WITH WOMEN OF FAITH

LYNN DOMINA

I0901717

JUDSON PRESS
PUBLISHERS SINCE 1824
VALLEY FORGE, PA

DEVOTIONS FROM HERSTORY: 31 DAYS WITH WOMEN OF FAITH

Judson Press has made every effort to trace the ownership of all quotes. In the event of a question arising from the use of a quote, we regret any error made and will be pleased to make the necessary correction in future printings and editions of this book.

Interior and cover design by Wendy Ronga, Hampton Design Group.

Library of Congress Cataloging-in-Publication data
Cataloging-in-Publication Data available upon request.
Contact cip@judsonpress.com.

Printed in the U.S.A.

First printing, 2019.

For Rev. Teressa Sivers,
who inspired this book
and so much else

Contents

Preface

Women's History Month is celebrated in the United States every March. Organizers chose March to coincide with International Women's Day on March 8, which was celebrated for the first time in 1911. During the late 1970s, school districts, colleges, and other organizations began to celebrate Women's History Week, and President Jimmy Carter first declared National Women's History Week in 1980. The next year and for several years after, Congress also issued proclamations supporting National Women's History Week. In 1987, the week was expanded to a month. Its purpose has been to highlight the contributions of women to society, not only in the private sphere—as mothers, wives, sisters, and partners—but also in the public sphere—as teachers, judges, scientists, and artists. History courses and history books have often neglected these contributions, focusing instead on male generals and presidents, with a few famous women such as Betsy Ross or Florence Nightingale given only a sidebar.

Although the organization of activities related to Women's History Month has primarily been accomplished by secular institutions and groups, some churches also acknowledge the contributions of women during the month. Because the role of women in religion remains controversial within some denominations, and because, apart from Mary the mother of Jesus and perhaps Mary Magdalene, women in the Bible are also often neglected in lectionaries and sermons, it is important for religious people to recognize and celebrate the contributions of other women as well. Women's History Month provides us with an opportunity to do just that, intentionally expressing our gratitude for the multitudes of women who have brought us to this moment in the twenty-first century.

Introduction

> When the woman saw that she could not remain hidden, she came trembling; and falling down before him, she declared in the presence of all the people why she had touched him, and how she had been immediately healed.—Luke 8:47

Women have often remained hidden in history, including religious history, as the number of nameless women in the Bible demonstrates. Yet even nameless women can be honored, and their trust, faith, and actions can inspire us even when we don't know exactly who they were. We often do know the names and biographical details of women who have lived more recently, and we can commit ourselves to keeping their memories alive. This book attempts to honor many women who have come before us, as well as several who are our contemporaries.

The primary purpose of *Devotions from HERstory: 31 Days with Women of Faith* is to connect the stories of women across time and to be a resource for our own devotional lives. The thirty-one entries for thirty-one days permit readers to begin these devotions at any time of the year, reflecting on different women's contributions over the course of a month. The biblical women of faith are primarily

Hebrew or early Christian women but also include Egyptians and Samaritans. The historic women with whom they are paired include women of many faith traditions—Christian, Jewish, indigenous, and others—as well as various ethnic and national backgrounds. They range from women who made their most dramatic contributions when they were teenagers to those who made an impact in adulthood and even towards the end of their lives. I'm grateful for each one of them.

They have all contributed to history, but these devotions situate them differently in time, as part of HERstory, not by excluding the men in their and our lives but by focusing on the women. We understand stories differently when we interpret them through the eyes of different characters. This book helps us examine the past and the present through the experiences of specific women. Their situations might (or might not) be very different from our own, but their responses offer inspiration for us all.

I have enjoyed learning about all these women and composing these reflections. I hope that you will find them valuable.

Day 1

The man named his wife Eve, because she was the mother of all living. And the LORD God made garments of skins for the man and for his wife, and clothed them.... Now the man knew his wife Eve, and she conceived and bore Cain, saying, "I have produced a man with the help of the LORD." Next she bore his brother Abel. Now Abel was a keeper of sheep, and Cain a tiller of the ground.—Genesis 3:20-21; 4:1-2

Alice Waters is a woman who motivated significant change in her neighborhood, and eventually around the entire country, through a casual remark. She said simply that a school near her home looked like nobody cared about it. We can probably imagine that school in Berkeley, California, because so many schools in so many neighborhoods also look blighted. But the principal of Martin Luther King Jr. Middle School heard Alice's remark less as a complaint than as an offer. Together they, along with teachers and other volunteers, transformed a schoolyard into a garden where students could learn horticulture, arithmetic, and even cooking through hands-on study of the history and the use of ancient grains—all before they enjoyed the products of their labor in the school cafeteria.

Alice Waters recognized an opportunity and contributed to a practical change in her neighborhood, as well as inspiring joy and enthusiasm.

We often think of Eve as a symbol of impulse and disobedience, and we allow that one choice she made (along with Adam) to eat the forbidden fruit to define her. Her choice does reveal part of her character, but that one act doesn't equal her entire being. She is, as Genesis tells us, "the mother of all living." She helped create new life, just as she had been created in the image of God. We can remember her as a woman who loved her garden and mothered her children, teaching them how to raise crops and tend herds. We can remember her as a woman who made a mistake and also as a woman who cultivated new growth.

Today's Question

What new growth have you cultivated?

God of growth,
help us see our world
as abundant and filled
with potential. Help us trust
our imaginations as we seek
to create new life
in places that seem forsaken.
Give us joy as we labor
in gardens and fields,

keeping our hope fresh
with the sprouting
of each new seedling.

Today's Action

Plant a packet of seeds indoors or outdoors as weather permits or start a new plant from a clipping of a houseplant.

Alice Waters (1944-)

Alice Waters was born in New Jersey. She attended college in California during the turbulent 1960s. As a young adult, she traveled in Europe and the Middle East, studying culinary practices. She focused particularly on the use of fresh foods. She also received training in a Montessori school, and the combination of Montessori education and culinary training influenced her later work introducing schoolchildren to gardening and cooking. Working with schoolchildren, she developed the concept of an "edible schoolyard," where students grow vegetables that are served in their cafeterias. Since the first edible schoolyard project was developed in California, the concept has spread across the country. In 1971 she opened a restaurant, Chez Panisse, which emphasizes the use of organic vegetables grown by local farmers. For her, food is a source of multiple types of sustenance, spiritual and social as well as physical. Food is a primary way of offering and receiving hospitality, and fresh, locally grown food has a more vibrant taste than food coated with pesticides and shipped hundreds of miles. In addition to her restaurant business, she has worked with the USDA to improve school lunches throughout the country. She has won numerous awards both as a chef and as an activist. She has been inducted into the California Hall of Fame, the New Jersey Hall of Fame, and the National Women's Hall of Fame. The author of several cookbooks and a memoir, *Coming to My Senses: The Making of a Counterculture Cook,* she lives in California.

Day 2

What woman having ten silver coins, if she loses one of them, does not light a lamp, sweep the house, and search carefully until she finds it? When she has found it, she calls together her friends and neighbors, saying, "Rejoice with me, for I have found the coin that I had lost."—Luke 15:8-9

Margaret "Maggie" Tobin Brown has become much better known by her posthumous nickname, the Unsinkable Molly Brown. A fictionalized version of her life was told in a play and then film, *The Unsinkable Molly Brown,* in which her character was played by Debbie Reynolds. Her character also appeared in the movie *Titanic,* played by Kathy Bates. Margaret Brown was one of the passengers on the *Titanic* who survived. Once in a lifeboat, she urged the crew to return to the ship to look for other survivors, many of whom were already in the water. With other women, she assisted in rowing the lifeboat. Her passion for helping others during this incident was consistent with other events in her life. Later, she was instrumental in forming a Survivor's Committee, raising funds for the support of impoverished survivors of the tragic shipwreck.

By the time she had sailed on the *Titanic*, Margaret Brown was a wealthy woman, but she had been raised in a working-class immigrant family in Missouri. Although her husband eventually earned a very good income as a mining engineer, she continued her service among poorer people, volunteering in a soup kitchen for miners' families and contributing to other philanthropic activities, especially those devoted to women. Just as the woman in Luke's story is known only as someone searching for what she has lost, Margaret Brown is remembered today, despite her many other accomplishments, for her attempts to save others in danger of being lost, drowned in the cold ocean.

Jesus' story in Luke is a parable rather than the rendering of an actual event, but we can easily imagine how thoroughly a poor woman would search for a misplaced coin. Her survival might depend on it. Because the story is a parable, the lost coin is both literal and symbolic, and we can apply the story to many aspects of our lives. Margaret Brown also understood how one person's survival might depend on another person's willingness to keep searching.

Today's Question

When you have felt most lost, how were you saved?

God who searches and saves,
remind us of your presence
when we feel tossed about
by life's unpredictability,
endangered by life's hazards.

When we are mired
in anxiety and uncertainty,
guide us back to you.
When we are secure and safe,
help us recognize
those who need our assistance.

Today's Action

Who most needs help in your community? Identify a morning or evening during the coming month when you could volunteer at a meal program, homeless shelter, hospice, literacy program, or some other service organization.

Margaret Tobin (Molly) Brown
(1867–1932)

Margaret Tobin Brown is known more colloquially as the Unsinkable Molly Brown. She was born in Hannibal, Missouri; her parents were Irish immigrants. As a young woman, she moved to Leadville, Colorado, with one brother, a sister, and a brother-in-law. Soon thereafter, she married James Brown, and they eventually had two children. A few years after their marriage, the Browns became quite wealthy (perhaps unexpectedly so) because of James's skills as a mining engineer. In addition to her cultural interests, Margaret also became engaged with philanthropic activities, especially those designed to assist families of miners.

She is most famous, however, as a passenger on the Titanic. Her presence aboard that ship was coincidental—she had been traveling in Europe and Africa when her grandson became seriously ill back in the United States. She booked passage on the first ship leaving for New York—the Titanic. Several lifeboats left the ship before they were completely full, and Margaret Brown repeatedly urged the crew of her lifeboat to return for more passengers. Subsequently she worked with other wealthy survivors to assist survivors who had been traveling on second- or third-class tickets. She used her subsequent fame to advocate for causes she believed in, including education, women's rights, and labor rights. She died in New York City from a brain tumor. As a result of continued fascination with the Titanic disaster, her life has been portrayed in several movies.

Day 3

The daughter of Pharaoh came down to bathe at the river, while her attendants walked beside the river. She saw the basket among the reeds and sent her maid to bring it. When she opened it, she saw the child. He was crying, and she took pity on him. "This must be one of the Hebrews' children," she said. Then his sister said to Pharaoh's daughter, "Shall I go and get you a nurse from the Hebrew women to nurse the child for you?" Pharaoh's daughter said to her, "Yes." So the girl went and called the child's mother. Pharaoh's daughter said to her, "Take this child and nurse it for me, and I will give you your wages." So the woman took the child and nursed it. When the child grew up, she brought him to Pharaoh's daughter, and she took him as her son. She named him Moses, "because," she said, "I drew him out of the water."—Exodus 2:5-10

Harriet Tubman is known as the American Moses, for she too brought many people—nearly seventy—out of slavery. As an escaped slave, she endangered herself by returning to slave territory thirteen times during the decade before the Civil War in order to lead others into freedom. Through her actions, she was able to reunite her family; they had been in danger of being sold apart from each other following their master's death. Geography contributed to Tubman's success. While she was enslaved, she lived in Maryland, so she could more easily slip into the free state of Pennsylvania than if she had lived farther south. She planned her trips carefully, often traveling during the winter when longer dark nights inhibited detection, and she sometimes imitated household workers in order to remain hidden in plain sight. During the Civil War itself, her work with the Union Army helped liberate hundreds more enslaved people.

Like Pharaoh's daughter, Harriet Tubman's compassion was stronger than her fear. Like Moses' sister Miriam, she often achieved her goals through ingenuity. As often occurs, the oppressed person outsmarted the oppressor. Neither Pharaoh's daughter nor Moses' sister nor Harriet Tubman could fully predict the momentous effects of their actions, yet they each still took action, led by hope and mercy.

Today's Question

When have you responded with goodness, even when you couldn't predict the success of your action?

God of mercy and hope and freedom,
give us the courage to choose
freedom for ourselves
and to model freedom for others.
Help us to recognize

choices that will enslave us
and to reject temptations
to oppress others.
Created in your image,
we strive to perceive
sparks of divinity
in each person we meet.
May those sparks
light our way to wholeness.

Today's Action

Write in your journal about the aspects of your life that are most freeing, as well as those that might still feel as if they are holding you captive.

Harriet Tubman (c. 1822–1913)

Harriet Tubman was born in Maryland as an enslaved person. She had several masters as a child. As a young woman, she escaped to Philadelphia, returning to slave territory on thirteen occasions to assist other enslaved people in their escapes, beginning with her family. She relied on the sophisticated system of the Underground Railroad, through which abolitionists would provide shelter and sometimes transportation to escaping slaves. She did not reveal the names of anyone who helped her or the details of any of her routes until several years after the

Civil War in order to protect abolitionists and continue to make it possible for enslaved people to escape by the same path she took. Because of these risky trips, she is known as the American Moses. Told Bible stories as a child, she became a Christian and was most attracted to the stories in the Book of Exodus that described the escape of the Israelites from their slavery in Egypt. In 1844, she married John Tubman, a free black man, though the relationship would soon dissolved. She was able to purchase property in Auburn, New York, in 1859, and she hosted family members at her home there. During the Civil War, she worked for the Union Army in several capacities, including as a spy. In 1869 she married Nelson Charles Davis, a veteran of the United States Colored Troops. That same year an acquaintance, Sarah Hopkins Bradford, published a biography called *Scenes in the Life of Harriet Tubman* in order to help alleviate some of Tubman's financial difficulties. As she aged, she grew frail and died of pneumonia in 1913. She is buried in Auburn, New York.

Day 4

In those days Mary set out and went with haste to a Judean town in the hill country, where she entered the house of Zechariah and greeted Elizabeth. When Elizabeth heard Mary's greeting, the child leaped in her womb. And Elizabeth was filled with the Holy Spirit and exclaimed with a loud cry, "Blessed are you among women, and blessed is the fruit of your womb. And why has this happened to me, that the mother of my Lord comes to me? For as soon as I heard the sound of your greeting, the child in my womb leaped for joy. And blessed is she who believed that there would be a fulfillment of what was spoken to her by the Lord."—Luke 1:39-45

Elizabeth Hooton lived in England during the seventeenth century and was among the earliest Quakers. Some sources suggest that she was the first person to be "convinced" after hearing the words of Quaker founder George Fox. Through the strength of her own convictions, she persuaded Fox that women could be called to ministry as authentically as men. Soon after she had become convinced of the truth of Fox's message, she began to hold meetings in her home so that others could hear him. Hooton is celebrated today for her work as a missionary who traveled on several occasions to North America to support Quakers in New England. She died in 1672 after traveling to Jamaica and nursing George Fox back to health on that trip.

Sometimes God speaks to us directly, during prayer or meditative reading. Other times, God speaks to us through nature, life events, or the voices of other people. Both Elizabeth Hooton and Mary's relative Elizabeth recognized the truth through hearing the words of another person. Elizabeth Hooton likely heard George Fox preach about the validity of each person's inner light and the importance of conversion. Mary's cousin Elizabeth needed to hear only Mary's greeting before she recognized the truth. Both women then proclaimed their experience. Their common experience confirms that God does approach each of us, yet their distinct experiences also reveal that God speaks to each of us in a unique voice.

Today's Question

Through whom, and in what ways, does God speak to you?

God of friendship and family,
you have blessed us with the power to speak
and to hear. Help us to recognize
your words, your will, your hope
in whichever voice expresses it.
Keep us grateful for all voices

that express your truth.
Give us the courage to respond,
revealing to others the Good News we have heard.

Today's Action

Write a letter to your local newspaper or another periodical, expressing support for a group of people or organization in your community.

"The Love I bear to the Souls of all Men,
makes me willing to undergo whatever
can be inflicted on me."

Elizabeth Hooton (1600–1672)

Born in Nottingham, England, Elizabeth Hooten was one of the earliest Quakers. Little is known of her early life, aside from the fact that she married Oliver Hooton and gave birth to several children. She met George Fox, the founder of the Religious Society of Friends, or Quakers, in 1647 and became convinced by his teachings. Her shifting beliefs created tensions in her marriage when her husband resisted her call to preach, though it was Elizabeth Hooton's call that convinced George Fox that women could be called equally with men. Unusual for her time, she could both read and write. She wrote and published religious pamphlets, and many of her letters have survived, including one to King Charles II. Like many early Quakers, she was imprisoned in England

and also persecuted when she traveled to the American colonies. Her trips to the New World occurred after she was sixty years old, and when she was seventy-one she agreed to accompany Fox to Jamaica. Fox fell ill on the trip, and Hooton nursed him back to health. Once in Jamaica, Hooton herself fell ill and died only a week after they landed. Following her death, George Fox commented that "Elizabeth Hooton, a woman of great age, who had travelled much in Truth's service, and suffered much for it, departed this life. She was well the day before she died, and departed in peace, like a lamb, bearing testimony to Truth at her departure."

Day 5

> Then the servant took ten of his master's camels and departed, taking all kinds of choice gifts from his master; and he set out and went to Aram-naharaim, to the city of Nahor. He made the camels kneel down outside the city by the well of water; it was toward evening, the time when women go out to draw the water. And he said, "O LORD, God of my master Abraham, please grant me success today and show steadfast love to my master Abraham. I am standing here by the spring of water, and the daughters of the townspeople are coming out to draw water."—Genesis 24:10-13

Rosie the Riveter is a composite character representing women who went to work in American factories during World War II. While historians have preserved the names of some of the women whose work influenced the portrayal of the iconic woman wearing a bandana and flexing her muscle with her sleeve rolled up, many of these women are unknown to us today. They accepted their government's encouragement to enter the workforce when their husbands, brothers, and sons fought overseas, and they most often relinquished their jobs when the men returned. Within a few decades, assumptions about gender roles would shift dramatically in the United States, but in the late 1940s, most women represented by Rosie the Riveter resumed their conventional tasks.

In this passage from Genesis, Abraham's servant has returned to Abraham's ancestral homeland to find a wife for Isaac. He is concerned that he won't recognize the proper wife and that none of the women will be willing to return with him to Canaan. A few verses after this passage, Rebekah appears with a group of women, performing her ordinary chores. She is among this group of ordinary anonymous women, yet she becomes a matriarch of Israel, mother to Jacob and Esau, and ancestor of all of their descendants.

Like the anonymous women in the passage from Genesis, women represented by Rosie the Riveter accomplished the work prescribed for women. Almost all this work is necessary, and some of it is meaningful for many women. Yet other women find these tasks confining or even deadening. In the best of circumstances, our work contributes to our life's purpose and also improves the lives of others. Good work can be very satisfying, whether it is performed in our home or in a school, in a courtroom or some other public place, whether it is paid or unpaid, whether it is traditional or something entirely new.

Today's Question

How do you decide when to accept, and when to resist, the roles thrust upon you?

O God our God,
who works to create
and sustain the world,
give us each meaningful work.
Provide work for us
so that we may provide
sustenance for one another.
Encourage us to cultivate
our talents, developing them
for the benefit of all.

Today's Action

Pray for those who do not have enough work and for those whose work is deadening to their spirits.

Rosie the Riveter

Rosie the Riveter is a composite fictional character created in 1943 to honor women who worked in factories during World War II. When the image was created by artist J. Howard Miller, its purpose was to persuade women to accept jobs in manufacturing, particularly those directly related to defense, as their patriotic duty because so many men had been drafted or volunteered for military service. If the Allies hoped to win the war, women needed to assume some of the responsibilities previously reserved for men. The needs of the nation were presented as greater than any individual woman's desire to maintain a traditionally feminine role, and women were encouraged to work outside the home while simultaneously fulfilling a culturally approved value—patriotism. At the time, much commentary on the image assured viewers that women could work in factories and simultaneously retain their feminity. The woman in the poster wears make-up and has polished fingernails—she's presented as tougher than the enemy but also attractive enough for an American husband or boyfriend. As American culture changed over the course of the 20th century, different aspects of her character would be emphasized. Following Miller's creation, Norman Rockwell painted her image for a cover of *The Saturday Evening Post;* Rockwell's version has attained iconic status. Before the war ended, Redd Evans and John Jacob Loeb wrote a song titled "Rosie the Riveter," which further sealed her cultural significance. Her image is currently reproduced widely, not as a specifically patriotic figure but as a way of promoting women's achievements and encouraging women to accomplish more than they might think they're capable of.

Day 6

Now in Joppa there was a disciple whose name was Tabitha, which in Greek is Dorcas. She was devoted to good works and acts of charity. At that time she became ill and died. When they had washed her, they laid her in a room upstairs. Since Lydda was near Joppa, the disciples, who heard that Peter was there, sent two men to him with the request, "Please come to us without delay." So Peter got up and went with them; and when he arrived, they took him to the room upstairs. All the widows stood beside him, weeping and showing tunics and other clothing that Dorcas had made while she was with them. Peter put all of them outside, and then he knelt down and prayed. He turned to the body and said, "Tabitha, get up." Then she opened her eyes, and seeing Peter, she sat up. He gave her his hand and helped her up. Then calling the saints and widows, he showed her to be alive.—Acts 9:36-41

Victoria Leigh Soto had turned twenty-seven years old just a month earlier. On December 14, 2012 she was teaching first grade, as she had done nearly every day that fall. Her pupils were undoubtedly looking forward to the approaching holidays. Then Adam Lanza, twenty years old and apparently mentally ill, entered Sandy Hook Elementary School and began shooting. Victoria Soto hid her students in the closet, and when Lanza entered her classroom, she claimed that the children were in the auditorium. Eventually Lanza killed twenty students and six staff members, including Soto. She has been hailed as a hero because of her selfless efforts to save the children.

Victoria Soto was not raised from the dead as Peter raised Tabitha. Like all of those who were killed that day, she was mourned and memorialized, and her name continues to evoke grief. Our faith tells us that death is not the end, yet we still find ourselves wishing that those we've loved could be raised up and restored to us in this life.

Today's Question

How can we live so as to honor those who have died?

God of resurrection,
you've promised us
that those who mourn
shall be comforted.
Be with those who grieve,
those who suffer violence,
and those who commit it.
Lead us to extend comfort
when we witness sorrow,
and help us to receive comfort

when we have lost
all hope of solace.

Today's Action

Donate your time to a local school activity or purchase supplies for a local teacher.

Victoria Leigh Soto (1985–2012)

Victoria Leigh Soto was born in Bridgeport, Connecticut. Her father was Puerto Rican, and her mother's side of the family was of Irish descent. She grew up in a middle-class family, with her father working for the Connecticut Department of Transportation and her mother working as a nurse. The family had three other children. Victoria Soto attended Eastern Connecticut State University in order to become a teacher, majoring in education and history and graduating with high honors. At the time of her death, she was pursuing a master's degree. She taught first grade at Sandy Hook Elementary School and was one of the six adults murdered by Adam Lanza. When the shooting started, Soto instructed her students to hide in the closet. When some of the children ran from the closet, Soto threw herself on top of them, shielding them from the bullets and sacrificing her life. She is buried in Union Cemetery in Stratford, Connecticut. Following her death, Eastern Connecticut State

University established a scholarship in her honor. The new elementary school in Sandy Hook is named for her. In 2013, Soto, along with the other adult staff members who died that day, were posthumously awarded the Presidential Citizens Medal.

Day 7

God said to Abraham, "As for Sarai your wife, you shall not call her Sarai, but Sarah shall be her name. I will bless her, and moreover I will give you a son by her. I will bless her, and she shall give rise to nations; kings of peoples shall come from her."—Genesis 17:15-16

An enrolled member of the Menominee Native American Nation, Verna Fowler grew up on the reservation in Wisconsin, where she was encouraged to commit herself to helping others. In 1970 she lobbied for the Menominee Restoration Act, which granted federal recognition to the Menominee tribe and opened a way for its members to formally unite and exercise sovereignty over their land and life together. Recognizing that few Menominee people had the opportunity to pursue higher education despite their enthusiasm for doing so, she eventually accepted a call to help found the College of Menominee Nation and become its first president in 1993. Although the college remains small, well over a thousand students have graduated. Due to Verna Fowler's work on and off the reservation as an elementary- and secondary-school teacher and higher education administrator, many Native American children can hope for a better future.

Like Sarah, Verna Fowler invigorated a nation. The way was often uncertain for both women, but each one trusted her call, and for each, hope proved stronger than fear. Many of our own blessings have probably been made possible by people we might not even know or remember, yet we can still express our gratitude for their generosity. Their actions, founded in trust, can serve as models for all of us.

Today's Question

What would it mean for each and every of us to be a blessing for a nation?

God of all peoples,
remind us that we are blessed
and that we are called to be a blessing.
Help us to recall those who have come before,
making our lives possible,
and to remember that those
who will come after us
depend on our actions, our decisions,
our energy for goodness
to fill their lives.

Today's Action

Write in your journal about anyone who has been a blessing to you. If that person is still living, write a thank-you note for his or her influence on your life.

Verna Fowler (1942-)

Verna Fowler was born on a Menominee reservation in Wisconsin, where she grew up. After she graduated from a Catholic high school and attended college, she joined the Franciscan order whose sisters had staffed her elementary school. In 1980 she, along with several other women, founded a new type of religious order called A New Genesis. Unlike in traditional women's orders, members of A New Genesis live and work independently of each other but gather occasionally for social interaction and spiritual growth. She is best known for her public work with the Menominee tribe. In 1970, she began to work with another tribal member to achieve federal recognition of the tribe, which was accomplished in 1973. She subsequently worked with the tribe to establish its tribal government. Recognizing that higher education was one of the Menominee's greatest needs, she agreed to start a new tribal college. The College of Menominee Nation opened its doors in 1993, and Fowler became its founding president. She retired from her role as president of the college in 2016, the same year she celebrated her fiftieth anniversary as a religious sister. She is co-author of a children's book, *The Menominee.* Under presidents Bill Clinton and George W. Bush, she served on the President's Board of Advisors on Tribal Colleges and Universities. She has also served on the boards of other national organizations related to higher education.

Day 8

A woman whose little daughter had an unclean spirit immediately heard about Jesus, and she came and bowed down at his feet. Now the woman was a Gentile, of Syrophoenician origin. She begged him to cast the demon out of her daughter. He said to her, "Let the children be fed first, for it is not fair to take the children's food and throw it to the dogs." But she answered him, "Sir, even the dogs under the table eat the children's crumbs." Then he said to her, "For saying that, you may go—the demon has left your daughter." So she went home, found the child lying on the bed, and the demon gone.—Mark 7:25-30

In her memoir *The Woman Warrior,* Maxine Hong Kingston reveals a secret story. The book opens with an instruction the narrator hears from her mother: "You must not tell anyone." But the narrator is disobedient, for she tells all her readers this shameful family secret. We're grateful that Kingston used her own judgment, persisting in her calling as a writer. Her story is memorable, and most readers end up sympathizing with the aunt whose story she tells, a woman who was cast out of the family. Kingston herself doesn't know the whole story, but she imagines its possibilities and helps her readers understand each of those possibilities.

Telling our stories can help heal us of shame, just as speaking back to those who insult us can deflect the shame they might hope we feel. Sometimes our circumstances are so dire that we have no choice but to persist. Many people are shocked by the behavior of Jesus in this passage. His statement not only sounds unkind but also prejudiced against all who aren't children of Israel. Nevertheless, when the woman persisted rather than retreat in shame, he healed her daughter. This unnamed woman's identity as a loving and desperate mother is more crucial to her than any other aspect of her identity. The Syrophoenician woman in Mark's Gospel loved her daughter so much that she risked further insult from Jesus and, through her persistence, revealed that his mission was to Gentiles as well as to Jews.

Today's Question

What stories are you called to tell? Who has called you to a fuller understanding of yourself?

God who spoke the world into being,
give us the courage to speak up
against neglect or discrimination or shame.
Help us remember
the value of our stories,
which are always part

of your great story.
Guide us to share our stories
and to hear the stories of others
so that we may all understand
our many connections.

Today's Action

Reveal something about yourself, something you've kept hidden, to someone you trust. In your journal, reflect on this experience. What was it like for you and for your confidante?

Maxine Hong Kingston (1940–)

Maxine Hong Kingston was born in Stockton, California. Her parents immigrated from China; her father arrived several years before her mother, who gave birth to Maxine in the first year of her U.S. residence. She married Earll Kingston in 1962, and they have one son. She graduated from the University of California—Berkeley, and as a young woman taught high school. She lived for a few years in Hawaii, where she wrote most of her first book, *The Woman Warrior: Memoirs of a Girlhood Among Ghosts,* which remains her best known. It combines fiction with nonfiction and memoir with mythology, making it an unusual and thought-provoking book. She has subsequently published several other books, primarily nonfiction. *The Woman Warrior* combines autobiography with mythology in order to show the influence of cultural stories on members of that culture. Although some Asian American writers have criticized Kingston for exaggerating negative aspects of Chinese culture, she has won numerous awards, including the National Book Award, the National Humanities Medal, and the National Medal of Arts. She has used her fame to become a public voice for peace, participating in anti-war demonstrations and other movements for women's rights during the early twenty-first century. Kingston taught for many years at the University of California—Berkeley, where she is now a professor emeritus.

Day 9

Thus says the LORD of hosts: Consider, and call for the mourning women to come; send for the skilled women to come; let them quickly raise a dirge over us, so that our eyes may run down with tears, and our eyelids flow with water. For a sound of wailing is heard from Zion: "How we are ruined! We are utterly shamed, because we have left the land, because they have cast down our dwellings." Hear, O women, the word of the LORD, and let your ears receive the word of his mouth; teach to your daughters a dirge, and each to her neighbor a lament.—Jeremiah 9:17-20

Rebecca Brown—often called Beckie—founded a chapter of Mothers Against Drunk Driving in northern Florida following the death of her son Marcus, who was killed by a drunk driver. She eventually served as national president of MADD. She channeled her grief into service and change. Judges and prosecutors began to approach the crime of driving while under the influence of alcohol more seriously. Public-service announcements began appearing on television. Friends began assigning one of their group as the designated driver, someone who would remain sober for the evening. Through the work of Brown and others, injuries and deaths due to drunk driving have been reduced significantly. Thousands of people are alive today because so many fewer intoxicated drivers are now endangering others. And many people who do drink alcohol have begun to do so much more responsibly, thanks to efforts of Beckie Brown and MADD.

The unnamed women in this passage from Jeremiah express grief because that is what they've been hired to do. Their activity formed part of their cultural tradition. We approach grief differently, sometimes privately and sometimes very publicly. Bringing grief into public awareness can contribute to positive change. By gathering with others who mourn and by publicly expressing their grief—and by telling the life stories of those who had been killed by drunk drivers—Beckie Brown influenced an entire nation to change its approach to driving under the influence.

Today's Question

How might we each use our grief for the benefit of others? How might we be consoled through our action in the world?

God of life,
you hear our grieving
and receive our mourning.
Help us to convert our sorrow
into hope
and our weeping

into promise.
Lead us to change our world
by changing ourselves,
saving ourselves,
and saving our children.

Today's Action

Write down the names of people you know whose lives have been affected by alcohol or other drugs. Pray for their healing.

Rebecca Brown (1940–2012)

Eighteen-year-old Marcus Brown died on December 9, 1979, when the car he was driving was hit by a drunk driver. Driving home from a party with her husband, Rebecca Brown, Marcus's mother, came upon the accident. Although the drunk driver was sentenced to eight years in prison, he served only two. Following the accident, Rebecca Brown committed herself to addressing the problem of drunk driving, which had not been taken seriously as a crime until Mothers Against Drunk Driving (MADD) was founded in 1980, even though thousands of people were killed as a result of drunk driving every year. Rebecca Brown founded the first chapter of Mothers Against Drunk Driving in Pasco County, Florida (on the Gulf Coast), and she participated in the foundation of the state chapter. She was eventually elected to the national

Board of Directors, and she served as national president from 1993 to 1995. Brown received numerous awards for her work. More importantly, as a result of her work and others like her, many people have begun to understand that accidents caused by drunk driving aren't just simply accidents but are the result of criminal behavior. People who drink alcohol have become much more conscious of their responsibilities, limiting the amount they drink if they plan to drive or choosing a friend as a "designated driver." The number of accidents and deaths attributable to drunk driving has decreased substantially in the years since MADD was founded.

Day 10

Mary [Magdalene] stood weeping outside the tomb. As she wept, she bent over to look into the tomb; and she saw two angels in white, sitting where the body of Jesus had been lying, one at the head and the other at the feet. They said to her, "Woman, why are you weeping?" She said to them, "They have taken away my Lord, and I do not know where they have laid him." When she had said this, she turned around and saw Jesus standing there, but she did not know that it was Jesus. Jesus said to her, "Woman, why are you weeping? Whom are you looking for?" Supposing him to be the gardener, she said to him, "Sir, if you have carried him away, tell me where you have laid him, and I will take him away." Jesus said to her, "Mary!" She turned and said to him in Hebrew, "Rabbouni!" (which means teacher). Jesus said to her, "Do not hold on to me, because I have not yet ascended to the Father. But go to my brothers and say to them, 'I am ascending to my Father and your Father, to my God and your God.'" Mary Magdalene went and announced to the disciples, "I have seen the Lord"; and she told them that he had said these things to her.—John 20:11-18

Rabbi Angela Warnick Buchdahl serves as senior rabbi at Central Synagogue in New York City. In some ways, she is a typical rabbi. As a child, she participated in temple activities, and she visited Israel through a youth program. She earned a degree in religion and studied at Hebrew Union College. She served as a cantor at Central Synagogue before becoming its senior rabbi. Yet in other ways, she is very unusual. Born in Korea, she immigrated with her family to the United States when she was five. Her mother had been born in Japan and practiced Buddhism. Her father was a Russian Jew of Romanian descent. Angela Buchdahl is the first Asian American to be ordained a rabbi. Because of her appearance and ancestry, she challenges expectations and many people's stereotypes of who a rabbi might be, just as Mary Magdalene challenged expectations by being the first to witness and proclaim the risen Christ.

Mary Magdalene lived during a time when leadership roles were almost always reserved for men. She would not have been easily recognized as an evangelist, bringing good news to the disciples. Because Judaism has historically been an ethnic religion that does not actively seek converts, Rabbi Buchdahl is also an unexpected image of a religious leader; yet she, too, brings messages of hope and promise to her congregation.

Today's Question

When has God startled you into paying attention by choosing an unexpected messenger?

God our teacher,
we are grateful for your message
and your messengers.
Guide us to see past
our own expectations and to listen
for your voice within the clamor and quiet
of our lives. After we have seen
and heard and believed,
lead us to also be effective messengers,
assisting those who still long
to experience your loving kindness.

Today's Action

Read an article or book about a religion or culture different from your own.

Angela Warnick Buchdahl (1972–)

Angela Warnick Buchdahl was born in Seoul, South Korea. Her mother had been born in Japan, immigrated to Korea, and practiced Buddhism; her father was of Romanian and Russian descent and an Ashkenazi Reform Jew. The family immigrated to the United States when Angela was five. They lived in Tacoma, Washington, where Angela was raised Jewish and became actively involved in the local synagogue. When she was sixteen, she visited Israel with a group of Jewish teenagers. There, for the first time, her identity as Jewish was questioned because of her Asian ancestry and because her mother wasn't Jewish. (Orthodox Judaism traces descent through a child's mother for the purpose of religious identity; other branches of Judaism are more flexible on this issue.) Returning to the United States, Buchdahl attended Yale University and graduated with a Bachelor of Arts in Religious Studies. She enrolled at Hebrew Union College to study to be a cantor and rabbi. After her ordination, she served as cantor and eventually as rabbi at Central Synagogue in New York City. She was elevated to Senior Rabbi in 2014, the first woman and the first Asian American to hold that post. She was, in fact, the first Asian-American to serve as a cantor at any synogogue in the world. She has been interviewed on radio and television and been listed among the most influential rabbis in the United States. She currently lives with her husband and children in New York City.

Day 11

At that time Deborah, a prophetess, wife of Lappidoth, was judging Israel. She used to sit under the palm of Deborah between Ramah and Bethel in the hill country of Ephraim; and the Israelites came up to her for judgment.—Judges 4:4-5

Sonia Sotomayor serves as an Associate Justice of the United States Supreme Court. Before joining the Supreme Court in 2009, she worked as a prosecuting attorney and civil litigator, as well as a U.S. District Court judge. She has been required to rule on cases involving civil rights, property rights, freedom of speech, and major league baseball and football. More so than many of her colleagues, Sotomayor makes frequent public appearances, often by giving commencement addresses and other speeches at universities. But she also chooses to interact with ordinary people in less serious contexts. She has twice appeared as a guest on *Sesame Street,* for example, explaining to children what occurs in a courtroom and how a judge decides a case. In 2013 she appeared at the festive celebration of New Year's Eve in Times Square, leading the countdown of the last seconds of the year as the glittering ball dropped, signaling the beginning of 2014. Her choices reveal that judges can be just like the rest of us ordinary people.

The prophetess Deborah served as a judge for Israel during the period before Israel had a king. Judges were understood to be more prudent and to act with less self-interest than kings. She witnessed how oppressively the Canaanite king was treating the people of Israel, so she encouraged a man named Barak to lead soldiers in defense of Israel. Following this battle, the people of Israel experienced forty years of peace. Like Deborah, Sonia Sotomayor accepts her responsibility as a judge by interacting with the people around her. Although many of us may be called to jury duty once or several times in our lives, few of us will earn the title "judge." Yet we often judge one another and ourselves, and we sometimes need to remind ourselves to temper our judgements with mercy.

Today's Question

How can we restrain ourselves from judging others unnecessarily or unfairly?

God our judge,
open our eyes that we may see
opportunities for justice.
Open our ears that we may hear
pleas for mercy.
Lead us to protect the vulnerable,
including ourselves,
and challenge the powerful,

including ourselves.
Give us wisdom,
that each of our decisions
may be fair and conscientious and compassionate.

Today's Action

Become informed about an important legal debate or controversy in your community so that you can contribute to a just resolution.

Sonia Sotomayor (1954–)

Sonia Sotomayor was born in the Bronx, a borough of New York City, of Puerto Rican parents. Her father died when she was nine. She has one younger brother. Her family spoke Spanish in their home, and she didn't become fluent in English until she was ten years old. She attended Princeton as an undergraduate, majoring in history and encouraging the university to engage with diversity both in its curriculum and its hiring. Subsequently, she attended Yale Law School, earning her degree in 1979. Following law school, she worked as an assistant district attorney in New York. She later practiced civil law and served on several boards that oversaw such things as tenants' rights and campaign finance. She was eventually nominated to a federal judgeship for the U.S. District Court and then for the U.S. Circuit Court. President Barack

Obama nominated her to the United States Supreme Court and following her confirmation hearings she was sworn in on August 8, 2009. She is the first Supreme Court Justice of Hispanic heritage, and only the third woman to serve on the Court. She is also only one of fourteen Catholic justices in the Supreme Court's history. In 2013 she published a memoir, *My Beloved World*, that covers both her childhood and adult life. She has received numerous honorary law degrees and other honors. She lives in Washington, DC.

Day 12

[Jesus] entered a certain village, where a woman named Martha welcomed him into her home. She had a sister named Mary, who sat at the Lord's feet and listened to what he was saying. But Martha was distracted by her many tasks; so she came to him and asked, "Lord, do you not care that my sister has left me to do all the work by myself? Tell her then to help me." But the Lord answered her, "Martha, Martha, you are worried and distracted by many things; there is need of only one thing. Mary has chosen the better part, which will not be taken away from her."—Luke 10:38-42

When Poland was invaded by the Nazis early in World War II, Stefania Podgórska was only fourteen years old, while her sister, Helena, was ten years younger. Their father had died in 1938, and their mother and brother were conscripted as forced laborers for the Nazis. Stefania worked as a clerk in a grocery store owned by a Jewish family until they were removed to a Jewish ghetto. As the Holocaust became increasingly terrifying, the two girls harbored thirteen Jewish people in the attic of their apartment, including Stefania's former employers and their family and friends, who had escaped from the ghetto as they were about to be deported to concentration camps. All of these people survived the war. The Podgórska sisters were forced to think and act quickly at a young age, yet they demonstrated a rare maturity and determination.

One way of reading the story of Martha and Mary from Luke's Gospel is that contemplation is preferable to action. Another way of reading it is that some circumstances call for contemplation, for listening, for stillness; others call for active response. We don't always have the opportunity Mary had, to sit and listen to Jesus; sometimes we must do the work that Martha took on. But if we have made a practice of listening for God, we can assure ourselves that when the time comes for action, we will be guided toward the right choice. The Podgórska sisters made the right, though dangerous, choice, but they wouldn't have had such courage if they hadn't already thought about ethics and justice.

Today's Question

What actions have you been able to take because you have listened for God?

God of relationship,
we know that you are with us
each day. Help us to remember
your presence. Remove our distractions
so that we may rest in you,
in contemplation and in action. Guide us

toward compassion and courage
for the protection
of our sisters and brothers,
our friends and neighbors,
and the strangers in our midst.

Today's Action

Set aside twenty to thirty minutes for meditative prayer, waiting for God's guidance, and listening—only listening—quietly for whatever God will reveal.

Stefania and Helena Podgórska (1925–;1935–)

Stefania and Helena (pictured far left) Podgórska were sisters in a large Polish family. The family was Catholic. In 1939, a year after the death of their father, Stefania (also known as Fusia) moved with another sister from Lila, Poland to Przemysl, where she worked in a grocery store owned by the Diamants, a Jewish family. In 1941, the Germans occupied Przemysl, forcing all Jews into a ghetto, and Stefania and Helena's mother and brother were sent into forced labor in Germany. As a result, Stefania cared for Helena for the duration of the war. When rumors reached them that local Jews would be killed, the Podgórska sisters hid thirteen Jewish people in their home. All of them survived the war. In 1961, Stefania moved to the United

States and married Josef Diamant, whose family had owned the grocery store in Poland. They had two children. Helena remained in Poland and become a physician. In 1979, Yad Vashem, Israel's holocaust memorial, recognized the two sisters as among the Righteous Among the Nations, and Stefania participated in the opening of the United States Holocaust Memorial Museum. Some of the Jewish people who were hidden by the Podgórska sisters were reunited with them in 1995. Stefania currently lives in California, while Helena continues to live in Poland.

Day 13

When morning dawned, the angels urged Lot, saying, "Get up, take your wife and your two daughters who are here, or else you will be consumed in the punishment of the city." But he lingered; so the man seized him and his wife and his two daughters by the hand, the LORD being merciful to him, and they brought him out and left him outside the city. When they had brought them outside, they said, "Flee for your life; do not look back or stop anywhere in the Plain; flee to the hills, or else you will be consumed."… Then the LORD rained on Sodom and Gomorrah sulfur and fire from the LORD out of heaven; and he overthrew those cities, and all the Plain, and all the inhabitants of the cities, and what grew on the ground. But Lot's wife, behind him, looked back, and she became a pillar of salt.—Genesis 19:15-17,24-26

Zora Neale Hurston was a novelist and anthropologist. Her most widely read book is *Their Eyes Were Watching God,* a novel about Janie, a young girl who grows into womanhood, learning how to love others and herself. Much of Hurston's work, however, was folklore. Through her conversations with friends and strangers, Hurston preserved cultural stories that would likely have been forgotten. These stories are often highly imaginative, revealing the values of the communities that treasured them. Despite the professional respect she earned as a young woman, however, Zora Neale Hurston died in isolation and was buried in an obscure grave, forgotten by nearly everyone until many years later when another writer, Alice Walker, purchased a headstone for her grave.

Perhaps Lot's wife also wished to memorialize her community, looking back because she was already grieving her friends and neighbors who were dying. Although she is often reduced to a symbol of disobedience, perhaps her disobedience was the result of her compassion. Perhaps she had loved her neighbors despite their flaws and hoped to see them saved. What if we were to honor her story, to bring the unnamed wife of Lot back from obscurity?

Today's Question

What if we treasured the past, even those parts we wish had been different?

God of relationships,
help us to know what to save
and what to relinquish.
When we must flee
for our lives,
keep us safe.

When we are safe,
give us courage
to receive those running from danger,
to protect them, to listen
as they tell their stories.

Today's Action

Take some flowers to the grave of a family or community member who is close to being forgotten.

Zora Neale Hurston (1891-1960)

Zora Neale Hurston was born in Alabama, but her family moved to Eatonville, Florida, when she was three years old. Eatonville was an all-black town, which meant that leadership positions, from mayor to minister (and her father served as both), were held by black people. Hurston, therefore, grew up with different assumptions about what was possible for her than did many African American people of her generation. Hurston attended Howard University, Barnard College, and Columbia University, studying with anthropologists Franz Boaz and Ruth Benedict. She traveled throughout the Deep South of the United States, as well as to Jamaica and Haiti, collecting folklore and conducting research on voodoo. She published collections of folk tales as well as an autobiography, but she is best known today for her novel

Their Eyes Were Watching God, part of which is set in a town like Eatonville. As a writer, Hurston is often classified as a participant in the Harlem Renaissance; she knew many of the other writers involved in that movement and collaborated with Langston Hughes, though they had a falling out over the production of their play, *Mule Bone.* Not long after *Their Eyes Were Watching God* was published, Hurston fell out of the public eye, and her work went out of print. She lived in poverty toward the end of her life. Following a stroke, she died in 1960 and was buried in an unmarked grave. Her work was brought back into print and a marker placed on her grave through the persistence of novelist Alice Walker. Her work remains very popular to this day.

Day 14

Now after [the wise men] had left, an angel of the Lord appeared to Joseph in a dream and said, "Get up, take the child and his mother, and flee to Egypt, and remain there until I tell you; for Herod is about to search for the child, to destroy him." Then Joseph got up, took the child and his mother by night, and went to Egypt, and remained there until the death of Herod.—Matthew 2:13-15a

Ruby Bridges was a little girl living in New Orleans, Louisiana, in 1954, when the Supreme Court ruled that school segregation was unconstitutional in the case of Brown v. Board of Education. Her parents had dreams for her future. They shared a hope that her life might be easier than theirs had been, that her opportunities might be greater than theirs. So they sent her to school. This ordinary act, however, placed her in such danger that she required an armed escort. That's because Ruby Bridges was black and her parents were sending her to a "white" school in a newly desegregated Louisiana. Some of the white citizens of New Orleans and other towns could not tolerate the possibility that white children and black children would sit beside one another. A hostile crowd surrounded Ruby as she walked down the sidewalk on her first day of school. They carried signs painted with hateful slogans. They threatened her. We can imagine her terror, just as we can imagine Mary's terror as she and Joseph tried to save their son.

Matthew's Gospel does not place much emphasis on Mary, but his is the only Gospel that tells this story of the flight into Egypt. Although the story focuses more on Joseph, we can imagine Mary, this new young mother, riding a donkey, perhaps walking, hurrying through the night as she held her child to her. We can imagine the hope she had for her son, the life she dreamed for him. We can imagine her wondering, who are these men who would do such a thing? Ruby's parents must have also wondered, who are these people who would do such a thing?

Today's Question

What have you done to protect a child in your life, whether your own or someone else's?

God our parent,
we long to hold our children close,
to stroke their cheeks
and curl their fingers around our own.
Be with us as we resist our culture
when it teaches us to hate.
Help us to recognize every child
as your child,

to value every child
as fiercely as we protect our own.

Today's Action

Look at some photographs of a child you care about or of yourself when you were a child. Let the photos evoke memories. Think about everything you've done to protect that child.

Ruby Bridges (1954–)

Born in Tylertown, Mississippi, Ruby Bridges moved with her family to New Orleans, Louisiana, when she was four years old. Two years later, in 1960, she became the first African American child to enroll in a previously all-white elementary school, William Frantz Elementary. The famous Supreme Court case, Brown v. Board of Education, had been decided just a few months before Ruby's birth, and schools throughout the South were struggling with its mandate. Ruby's mother was particularly invested in the integration of New Orleans schools, not only for the benefit of her own daughter but also for the good of all children. Throughout her first year, Ruby was escorted to school by federal marshals. Many white parents withdrew their children from the school, and only one teacher agreed to teach her. Six-year-old Ruby was threatened by white adults, and her family suffered significantly. Her father was fired from his job, and her grandparents were evicted from land they had sharecropped. On the second day of Ruby's attendance at William Frantz Elementary, however, one other white child joined her, and soon a few other white students followed. Robert Coles, famed child psychiatrist, met with her throughout her first year at William Frantz Elementary School and subsequently wrote *The Story of Ruby Bridges*. Bridges herself has written a book for children, *Through My Eyes,* which was published in 1999. That same year she created the Ruby Bridges Foundation, whose mission is to promote "the values of tolerance, respect, and appreciation of all differences." She has received numerous awards and has been honored by municipalities and organizations throughout the country. She continues to live in New Orleans, though her former home, like many others, was destroyed by Hurricane Katrina in 2005.

Day 15

> It happened, late one afternoon, when David rose from his couch and was walking about on the roof of the king's house, that he saw from the roof a woman bathing; the woman was very beautiful. David sent someone to inquire about the woman. It was reported, "This is Bathsheba daughter of Eliam, the wife of Uriah the Hittite." So David sent messengers to get her, and she came to him, and he lay with her.—2 Samuel 11:2-4a

At the age of fourteen, Elizabeth Smart was abducted from her home by Brian David Mitchell, who had a history of drug and alcohol abuse and criminal activity. He had previously worked for her family and believed himself to be a prophet. With the assistance of his wife, he held Elizabeth captive for nine months. After kidnapping Elizabeth, Mitchell performed a ceremony he deemed a marriage, although he deprived Elizabeth of any power of consent. While he held her captive, he raped her frequently. Eventually, Elizabeth was found and freed by police, and returned to her family. As an adult, she has advocated for victims with similar experiences.

When her captor appeared, Elizabeth Smart was probably both confused and terrified. The Bible doesn't provide us with Bathsheba's thoughts or feelings about David's command. Perhaps she was flattered, but she may well have been angry or afraid. What we do know is that she had no choice. She could not depend on safety or privacy in her home; she was subject to a powerful man who happened to observe her. Just as Bathsheba could not refuse the desires of the king, Elizabeth Smart could not refuse the force of a man who held a knife to her neck. Both men's reliance on force reveals how unjust and immoral their desires were.

Today's Question

What can we do to prevent the powerful from abusing the powerless and to create a world where women and girls will be safe?

God of power and protection,
open our eyes
to see your image in every face.
Assist us as we work to protect
our mothers, daughters, and sisters.
Help us safeguard
all children and recognize
when they are in danger.
Show us how to reject
power over others, and lead us
to share power
as we share all your good gifts.

Today's Action

Make a financial donation to or become active with an organization that improves and protects the lives of women or children or both.

Elizabeth Smart (1987–)

Elizabeth Smart was born in Salt Lake City, Utah, and would probably have lived an ordinary life were it not for a dramatic event that occurred when she was fourteen years old. She lived with her parents, sister, and four brothers in Salt Lake City. In June 2002, she was kidnapped by Brian David Mitchell, a local man who had worked for her family and broke into their home, threatening Elizabeth with the knife he carried if she made any noise. She was held captive by Mitchell and his wife, Wanda Ileen Barzee, until March 2003, when witnesses recognized her abductors from news reports. Her parents had kept her name and story in the news, in the hope that public awareness would lead to her return. Following her rescue, she testified before Congress in support of new laws intended to protect children from child predators. She has also urged schools and parents to provide sex education for children that emphasizes their self-worth. A Mormon, she has spoken about the role of her faith in helping her survive her ordeal. After graduating from Brigham Young University, she participated in Mormon mission service. She met her husband, Matthew Gilmour, during that experience. They married in 2012 and have two children. In 2013 Elizabeth Smart published *My Story,* a memoir of her experience, and in 2018, she published her second book, *Where There's Hope: Healing, Moving Forward, and Never Giving Up,* which focuses on healing from trauma and reclaiming one's life. Her abduction has been the subject of numerous articles and movies. She continues to work on issues related to child protection and gives frequent public presentations about these issues.

Day 16

Then one of the leaders of the synagogue named Jairus came and, when he saw Jesus, fell at his feet and begged him repeatedly, "My little daughter is at the point of death. Come and lay your hands on her, so that she may be made well, and live." So he went with him.... Some people came from the leader's house to say, "Your daughter is dead. Why trouble the teacher any further?" But overhearing what they said, Jesus said to the leader of the synagogue, "Do not fear, only believe." He allowed no one to follow him except Peter, James, and John, the brother of James. When they came to the house of the leader of the synagogue, he saw a commotion, people weeping and wailing loudly. When he had entered, he said to them, "Why do you make a commotion and weep? The child is not dead but sleeping." And they laughed at him. Then he put them all outside, and took the child's father and mother and those who were with him, and went in where the child was. He took her by the hand and said to her, "Talitha cum," which means, "Little girl, get up!" And immediately the girl got up and began to walk about (she was twelve years of age).—Mark 5:22-24a,35-42a

Pretty Shield was a medicine woman of the Crow Indians. Born before the reservation system was implemented, she lived into the mid-twentieth century. She had seven children, two of whom died as infants, and she also raised several grandchildren. As a medicine woman, she treated those who were suffering physically as well as psychologically and spiritually. As a grandmother, she worried that her children and grandchildren would encounter situations for which their traditions had not prepared them. Many of her grandchildren did survive, however, and told their own stories, learning and teaching from their traditions.

Like Jairus, Pretty Shield had to learn not to fear but to trust, even in the midst of dramatic change. For Jairus, Jesus was a new kind of prophet who might show him the way through fear and despair. Pretty Shield could have surrendered to despair, as her nation's entire way of life seemed to be destroyed. Like Jairus's daughter, her grandchildren had to be courageous enough to rise.

Today's Question

What do you most fear, and how does your faith help you lay down your fear?

God our teacher and healer,
give us the energy to teach,
the patience to learn,
the compassion to heal,

and the courage to be healed.
Turning to the past,
we honor our ancestors.
Facing the future,
we bless our descendants.
Living in the present,
we rest in you.

Today's Action

Write in your journal about a time when your faith helped you overcome fear.

Pretty Shield (1856–1944)

Pretty Shield was a traditional medicine woman and member of the Crow Nation in Montana. She was raised traditionally before the reservation system was implemented, though even then the tribe suffered many of the effects of colonialism. Her father died of smallpox when she was sixteen. Her tribe was nomadic, following the buffalo, which they hunted for food and other purposes. Pretty Shield married Goes Ahead, a Crow warrior with whom she had seven children (two died as infants). She also raised several of her grandchildren. By the time her grandchildren were born, the tribe had moved onto a reservation, and the last few decades of her life were marked by cultural confusion and grief. As a medicine woman, she healed members of her tribe with medicinal plants, knowledge that she passed down to her granddaughter. She died in Montana in 1944. She is remembered today primarily through an ethnography completed by Frank B. Linderman, who interviewed her about her early life during the 1930s and published the compilation of their conversations as *Pretty-shield, Medicine Woman of the Crow*. One of the granddaughters Pretty Shield raised, Alma Hogan Snell, also wrote a memoir, *Grandmother's Grandchild: My Crow Indian Life*, in which she describes her childhood with Pretty Shield.

Day 17

But Ruth said,
Do not press me to leave you
  or to turn back from following you!
Where you go, I will go;
  where you lodge, I will lodge;
your people shall be my people,
  and your God my God.
Where you die, I will die—
  there will I be buried.
May the LORD do thus and so to me,
  and more as well,
if even death parts me from you!"

When Naomi saw that she was determined to go with her, she said no more to her. So the two of them went on until they came to Bethlehem.—Ruth 1:16-19a

Mildred Norman Ryder adopted the name Peace Pilgrim in 1953, when she was forty-four years old. In 1952, she had become the first woman to hike the entire Appalachian Trail in a single season, and she had already committed herself to inner peace and social action. On January 1, 1953, she declared her new name to be Peace Pilgrim and began another walk—from southern California to New York City. She hoped not only to preach peace but to enact it, trusting in the generosity of others for food and shelter. She recognized that peace begins within a person and firmly believed that peace in the world will not be achieved if individuals do not cultivate inner peace, often by simplifying their material lives. Unlike in many traditional pilgrimages during which people travel to sacred sites, her goal wasn't a spot on a map but an attitude, a way of being in the world. Similar to traditional pilgrimages, however, her most important insights occurred along the way rather than at its end. Her goal wasn't so much to arrive somewhere but to help the world change, individual by individual, step by step.

Mildred Ryder made an unusual decision, just as Ruth had in accompanying Naomi, a woman of a different culture and ethnic group with no living husband or sons to provide for her. Ruth's loyalty transcended difference. Like Ruth, Mildred Ryder walked, and she walked, and she walked, open to companionship, doing what she believed to be right, without insisting upon the attention of others.

Today's Question

When have you accompanied someone else on an uncertain journey?

God our peacemaker,
you have assured us that peacemakers

will be blessed.
As we walk on our way,
keep us mindful of one another.
Send us companions
for our journeys, and guide us
to friends who will plant peace
in each of our footprints.

Today's Action

Go for a walk around your neighborhood, noticing signs of goodness and greeting those you meet with compassion.

Mildred Norman Ryder (Peace Pilgrim) (1908–1981)

Mildred Norman Ryder was born in Egg Harbor City, New Jersey. Her family was comparatively poor, though not destitute. When she was twenty-five years old, she married Stanley Ryder, although they divorced thirteen years later. She achieved many physical accomplishments, such as hiking the entire Appalachian Trail, but she is most known as Peace Pilgrim because of her pilgrimages across the United States, speaking to people about peace. She had developed a spiritual practice of meditation, and during one of her sessions, she received a mystical insight that inspired her to start walking for peace. Though she had been exceptionally physically active, her decision to walk across America was founded in her spiritual practice rather than in any desire for a physical challenge. She began walking on January 1, 1953, and crossed the country seven times. She took with her only what she could carry in her pockets, accepting gifts of food when they were offered, fasting if they weren't. Along the way, she would speak at churches and universities and was interviewed on radio and television programs. She wrote an autobiography, *Peace Pilgrim: Her Life and Work in Her Own Words,* which was published posthumously in 1992. She died in 1981 in Indiana while being driven, ironically, to a speaking engagement. Her ashes were buried in a cemetery in her hometown.

Day 18

> [Jesus] sat down opposite the treasury, and watched the crowd putting money into the treasury. Many rich people put in large sums. A poor widow came and put in two small copper coins, which are worth a penny. Then he called his disciples and said to them, "Truly I tell you, this poor widow has put in more than all those who are contributing to the treasury. For all of them have contributed out of their abundance, but she out of her poverty has put in everything she had, all she had to live on."—Mark 12:41-44

Temple Grandin is internationally known as the voice of autism. Although she wasn't formally diagnosed with autism until she was in her forties, Grandin's mother hypothesized that Grandin had autism. Grandin didn't begin speaking until she was almost four years old, after intensive therapy provided by her mother and another caregiver. At that time—and to some extent still today—many people assumed that those with autism were destined to lead isolated, painful, and unproductive lives. Yet despite the challenges language presented for her, Temple Grandin earned a PhD in animal science and became a professor at Colorado State University, where she developed more humane methods of treating livestock. Through her presentations, speeches, and filmed interviews, she has also contributed significantly to public understanding of an autistic person's experience.

Here in Mark's Gospel, Jesus helps the disciples understand the widow's experience. Surrounded by wealthier people, some of whom might be giving ostentatiously, the widow seems to give very little—yet she also gives everything. The amount she gives is minimal, but her generosity is profound.

Like the poor widow, Temple Grandin was once perceived by many as having little to offer. Yet she knew that her experience allowed her insights that most people could not receive. The characteristic that many people consider a disability became her most effective tool. In offering what she had, she improved the lives of many—animals as well as human beings.

Today's Question

How might we all learn to trust that the gifts we have are worth giving?

God of generosity,
teach us how to give with joy
and receive with gratitude.
Lead us into the confidence
of knowing that each of our gifts

is valuable.
Help us understand how to ask
for just enough,
so that no one sinks
under the burdens of too much wealth
and no one trembles
with the anxiety of too much poverty.

Today's Action

Make a list of your gifts and your weaknesses. Pray that God will show you how to use even your weaknesses for the good of others.

Temple Grandin (1947–)

Temple Grandin is known primarily for two things, one of which led to the other, though their relationship isn't immediately obvious: her autism and her work related to the ethical treatment of animals. She was born in Boston, Massachusetts, into a wealthy and highly accomplished family. Her family was Episcopalian, though Temple Grandin does not identify herself as a religious person. Despite developmental problems as a child, she wasn't formally diagnosed with autism until she was in her forties, though her family did seek treatment for her needs. During the 1950s, most children with her condition would have been institutionalized, but her mother was determined to keep her at home, so she hired caretakers and special teachers. She attended private schools during middle school and high school, although she found those years difficult, as do many students with special needs. One of her science teachers, though, took a special interest in her, and they kept in touch after Grandin graduated. She earned an M.S. from Arizona State University and a Ph.D. in animal science from the University of Illinois. Dr. Grandin has published dozens of academic articles on the humane treatment of animals in addition to over a dozen books, the most well-known being *Thinking in Pictures*. She has won numerous awards and been the subject of several magazine articles and television productions. She currently lives in Colorado and teaches at Colorado State University.

Day 19

Rebekah said to her son Jacob, "I heard your father say to your brother Esau, 'Bring me game, and prepare for me savory food to eat, that I may bless you before the LORD before I die.' Now therefore, my son, obey my word as I command you. Go to the flock, and get me two choice kids, so that I may prepare from them savory food for your father, such as he likes; and you shall take it to your father to eat, so that he may bless you before he dies." But Jacob said to his mother Rebekah, "Look, my brother Esau is a hairy man, and I am a man of smooth skin...." His mother said to him, "... Obey my word, and go, get them for me." So he went and got them and brought them to his mother; and his mother prepared savory food, such as his father loved. Then Rebekah took the best garments of her elder son Esau, which were with her in the house, and put them on her younger son Jacob; and she put the skins of the kids on his hands and on the smooth part of his neck. —Genesis 27:6-11,13-16

Dorothy Day is best known as a founder of the Catholic Worker movement, along with Peter Maurin. The movement began in 1933 with the publication of the *Catholic*

Worker newspaper, which sought to promote Christian pacifism and hospitality to the poor and forsaken, in order to "live in accordance with the justice and charity of Jesus Christ." Over the years the Catholic Worker movement has opened dozens of houses of hospitality for homeless people across the nation, in addition to offering retreats for volunteers to connect their activism with spiritual practices.

Having been raised in a largely secular home and becoming involved with the socialist movement as a journalist and activist, Day converted to Catholicism after a period of spiritual longing, and she strove to align the religious teachings she admired with her experiences of poverty. She aspired to live a life of service, dedicated to the love of all people. Yet she also evoked criticism for her previous alignment with communism and socialism, her opposition to war, her efforts for women's rights, and her conflicts with the Vatican.

She may seem to have little in common with Jacob's mother, Rebekah, who is notorious for deceiving her husband, Isaac, in order to advance the status of her favorite son (whom God had told her during her difficult pregnancy would take pride of place over his older twin). Although many of us might be uncomfortable with Rebekah's actions, as well as with some of Dorothy Day's, we can also look to them as women who asserted themselves in cultures that urged women to remain passive and silent.

Today's Question

How might your characteristics and convictions that sometimes make others uncomfortable be gifts from God?

God of action
and of contemplation,
lead us to discern right action
when action is required.
May our words, too,
be the right words
and our intentions
be the right intentions.
Help us each to create
in ourselves and of ourselves
a house of hospitality.

Today's Action

Make a special meal for your family, friends, or someone who needs companionship.

Dorothy Day (1897-1980)

Dorothy Day remains one of the most well-known American Catholics. She was born in Brooklyn, New York, and moved with her family to San Francisco and later to Chicago. As a young adult, she returned to New York, where she became involved in socialist political activities. She was romantically involved with a series of men and became pregnant; she terminated that pregnancy through an abortion, illegal at the time. She became pregnant a second time, in 1925, as her attraction to Catholicism was increasing. Her daughter, Tamar Teresa, was born on March 4, 1926. By this time, Day was attending Mass regularly, and she had her daughter baptized. The child's father could not adjust to Day's increasingly religious orientation. Their relationship ended, and Dorothy Day was baptized Catholic. She supported herself as a journalist, writing for both secular and religious periodicals. A few years later, she met Peter Maurin, who introduced her to Catholic social teaching and helped her understand her commitment to social reforms in theological terms. Day, Maurin, and others founded the Catholic Worker movement, which began with the newspaper, the *Catholic Worker,* in 1933. The movement developed into a loosely structured organization that operated houses of hospitality throughout the country. During the 1940s, Day experienced tension within and beyond the church due to her commitment to pacifism and workers' rights, especially when workers at Catholic cemeteries went on strike; Dorothy Day and the *Catholic Worker* supported the workers in opposition to the archdiocese. She published several books, the best-known being *The Long Loneliness: The Autobiography of the Legendary Catholic Social Activist.* She died and is buried in New York City. She has been considered for canonization as a saint.

Day 20

> There was a woman who had been suffering from hemorrhages for twelve years; and though she had spent all she had on physicians, no one could cure her. She came up behind him and touched the fringe of his clothes, and immediately her hemorrhage stopped.... When the woman saw that she could not remain hidden, she came trembling; and falling down before him, she declared in the presence of all the people why she had touched him, and how she had been immediately healed. He said to her, "Daughter, your faith has made you well; go in peace."—Luke 8:43-44,47-48

Henrietta Lacks died of ovarian cancer in 1951. An African American woman from a poor family, she had been treated at Johns Hopkins Hospital before her death. The cancer cells taken from her body were unusual because they reproduced so vigorously. Now known as HeLa cells (for *He*nrietta *La*cks), this cell line has been used by cancer researchers throughout the country and around the world. Innumerable cancer patients have benefitted from discoveries assisted by HeLa cells and have received treatments that Henrietta Lacks herself would not have been able to afford. Medical researchers benefitted professionally through experiments they conducted by relying on HeLa cells. Unfortunately, the Lacks family received neither credit nor financial remuneration from this research until very recently, following publication of the 2010 book *The Immortal Life of Henrietta Lacks*.

Until the woman with the hemorrhage was cured, she would have suffered physically and medically, of course, but also socially and spiritually. Her bleeding would have designated her as "unclean," and she would have been prohibited from interacting fully with others. Unlike the unnamed woman in Luke's Gospel, Henrietta Lacks was not cured of her affliction, nor was she treated respectfully by many of those with the power to help her. For decades, she remained nearly as anonymous as the woman with the hemorrhage. Lacks's story assures us that our lives do matter, often in ways we cannot predict. Her story reminds us, once again, of how often we fail to acknowledge the dignity of those whose lives touch our own.

Today's Question

How has your faith helped you find dignity?

God our creator
and creator of all that is good,
we thank you for everything healthy within us.
We ask you to heal what remains to be healed,
to bless us with courage enough to reach for what we need.

Help us to honor those
whose sickness has made us well.
We pray for a time
when no one's name will remain hidden,
as our names are never hidden from you.

Today's Action

Pray for those with incurable illnesses, asking that despite the weaknesses of their bodies, they will receive spiritual healing from God.

Henrietta Lacks (1920–1951)

Henrietta Lacks would have remained a footnote in medical textbooks were it not for the publication in 2010 of *The Immortal Life of Henrietta Lacks* by Rebecca Skloot, which tells the story of Lacks's life, her family, and the medical research facilitated by her cancer cells. Born in Virginia, Henrietta Lacks was a member of a large extended family. After her mother died during childbirth when she was four years old, Lacks lived with her grandfather. She married her cousin, David "Day" Lacks, in 1941 and had five children. Shortly after the birth of her last child, Lacks was diagnosed with cervical cancer. She was treated at a hospital affiliated with Johns Hopkins University because it was the only facility in Maryland, where she now lived with her family, that would treat black patients. She died from cervical cancer less than ten months after its diagnosis and was buried in an unmarked grave because of her family's financial struggles. During her treatment, healthy and cancerous cells were removed from her body without her knowledge or permission to be used for research purposes. The cancerous cells developed into what is known as "immortal" cell lines—they will reproduce indefinitely. Known as HeLa, for Henrietta Lacks, cells, they are still used for cancer research. Neither Henrietta Lacks nor her family was informed of the existence of these cells for several years. Nor were they compensated, despite the fact that the cell line led to significant financial gain for the researchers and for Johns Hopkins University. Her family, many of whom remained quite poor, wasn't even aware of the contributions these cells had made to medical research until Rebecca Skloot told them. Thousands of people over the last several decades have been treated through discoveries made with HeLa cells, but the case continues to raise ethical questions regarding patient rights and privacy.

Day 21

When the horses of Pharaoh with his chariots and his chariot drivers went into the sea, the LORD brought back the waters of the sea upon them; but the Israelites walked through the sea on dry ground. Then the prophet Miriam, Aaron's sister, took a tambourine in her hand; and all the women went out after her with tambourines and with dancing. And Miriam sang to them: "Sing to the LORD, for he has triumphed gloriously; horse and rider he has thrown into the sea."—Exodus 15:19-21

Although Julia Ward Howe was born into an influential New England family, she suffered several early losses, including the deaths of both of her parents by the time she was twenty years old. She educated herself independently by reading through her brother's library, and she circulated among many of the most influential writers and thinkers of the nineteenth century. Shortly before the Civil War, she published a collection of poetry, but she is best known for "The Battle Hymn of the Republic," which is set to the tune of another abolitionist song, "John Brown's Body." Subsequent to the publication of this hymn, Julia Ward Howe became one of the most famous women in America. Even if people aren't familiar with its author's name, most can recite at least one of the song's lines: "Mine eyes hath seen the glory of the coming of the Lord" or "Glory! Glory! Hallelujah! His truth is marching on!"

Like Miriam's song in the book of Exodus, "The Battle Hymn of the Republic" praises God for intervening in history to free people from slavery. Many enslaved people, in fact, had looked to the Book of Exodus as their own story of hope. While many Christians today regret the violence described in the Exodus and other biblical passages, as well as in more recent history, we nevertheless celebrate the release of people from bondage into freedom.

Today's Question

How have you been set free from those things that have held you in bondage?

God of justice,
we trust that you lead us
each day into freedom.
Give us the strength to resist
the ways we enslave ourselves
and the courage to recognize
our call to liberate one another.

Today's Action

If you are a musician, take some time to play your instrument or sing. If not, listen to a new piece of music.

Julia Ward Howe (1819-1910)

Julia Ward Howe was born into an influential family in New York City, which permitted her to meet well-known writers and politicians. Her family was rigidly Calvinist, but her wide reading introduced her to ideas that challenged some of these religious teachings. In 1843 she married Samuel Gridley Howe, a physician interested in social reform; they had six children and spent most of their married life in Boston. Their marriage, was marked by conflict, especially when Julia began to publish poetry advocating for women's rights and revealing some of the difficulties of her marriage. She is best known, however, for the patriotic song "The Battle Hymn of the Republic," set to the music of another then-popular song, "John Brown's Body," which commemorated the death of the abolitionist. "The Battle Hymn of the Republic" was published in *The Atlantic Monthly* in early 1862, when it had become apparent that the Civil War would last much longer than most had anticipated. Supporters of the Union quickly adopted the song, and it remained popular throughout the war—and into the present. Having achieved public recognition, Howe returned to her interests in women's rights, particularly suffrage, though she would not see that goal finally achieved nationwide with the ratification of the Nineteenth Amendment in 1920. She died of pneumonia in 1910 and is buried in Cambridge, Massachusetts. At her funeral, thousands of mourners sang "The Battle Hymn of the Republic."

Day 22

After this Paul left Athens and went to Corinth. There he found a Jew named Aquila, a native of Pontus, who had recently come from Italy with his wife Priscilla, because Claudius had ordered all Jews to leave Rome. Paul went to see them, and, because he was of the same trade, he stayed with them, and they worked together—by trade they were tent makers.... Now there came to Ephesus a Jew named Apollos, a native of Alexandria. He was an eloquent man, well-versed in the scriptures. He had been instructed in the Way of the Lord; and he spoke with burning enthusiasm and taught accurately the things concerning Jesus, though he knew only the baptism of John. He began to speak boldly in the synagogue; but when Priscilla and Aquila heard him, they took him aside and explained the Way of God to him more accurately.—Acts 18:1-3,24-26

Margaret Fell Fox is one of the founders of the Religious Society of Friends, commonly known as Quakers. She met George Fox in 1652 and became a convinced Quaker soon after she first heard him speak. Both George and Margaret were imprisoned for their religious beliefs, and Margaret suffered additional criticism for her habit of speaking publicly about her religious beliefs, rather than keeping silent as women were often taught to do. While in prison, she composed what is perhaps her most well-known piece of writing, a pamphlet citing Scripture to justify public religious activity by women. Margaret's first husband died in 1658, and she married George Fox in 1669. She outlived him but remained active in defending and clarifying Quaker beliefs until her own death in 1702.

In the story of Priscilla and Aquila from the Acts of the Apostles, Priscilla teaches with as much authority as Aquila. She assists Apollos in expanding his knowledge of the traditions of Jesus and other early Christians. Like Priscilla, Margaret Fell Fox worked collaboratively with her husband to instruct new believers in her faith. She accepted her call to teach and to preach despite social opposition, as many women have continued to do. She teaches us not to give social convention too much weight, but to gather our courage and trust our calls even when others disapprove.

Today's Question

When have you challenged social convention in order to do what you were called to do?

God of wisdom and surprise,
we know that you often choose
to do a new thing.
Remind us as you have reminded so many others

to be not afraid.
We hope that our own words
reflect your teaching
and ask that you bless each of us called to speak
and all of us called to listen.

Today's Action

Read a magazine article or blog entry about a passage in the Bible that interests you, so that you too may understand "the Way of God … more accurately."

Margaret Fell Fox (1614–1702)

Margaret Fell Fox, born Margaret Askew, was one of the founders of the Religious Society of Friends, or Quakers. She was born in Lancashire, England, and married Thomas Fell in 1632. Through this marriage, she had aristocratic status, unusual for Quakers. In 1652 George Fox visited the Fells, offering instruction on his religious ideas, that each person is created with an inner light, the light of Christ. Each person's conscience has valid authority, so no person need be subject to a priest or other type of religious hierarchy. Additionally, women could speak and teach as freely as men. Indeed, one of Margaret Fell Fox's pamphlets was titled "Women's Speaking Justified," which based its argument on Christian Scripture. Quaker meetings occurred frequently in the Fells's home, and Margaret began writing pamphlets promoting Quaker ideas. For many decades, Quakers were persecuted in England and in many of the American colonies. Margaret was arrested repeatedly, sometimes spending years in jail. Because of her social status, however, she was sometimes able to intercede for others who had been arrested for their beliefs. Thomas Fell died in 1658, and eleven years later, Margaret married George Fox, though they were often separated due to George's travels and both of their occasions of imprisonment. George Fox died in 1691, just as the English government was becoming more tolerant of Quakers. Margaret died at home and was buried in an unmarked grave, as was the Quaker practice, within a Quaker cemetery.

Day 23

Sarah saw the son of Hagar the Egyptian ... playing with her son Isaac. So she said to Abraham, "Cast out this slave woman with her son; for the son of this slave woman shall not inherit along with my son Isaac."... So Abraham rose early in the morning, and took bread and a skin of water, and gave it to Hagar, putting it on her shoulder, along with the child, and sent her away. And she departed, and wandered about in the wilderness of Beer-sheba. When the water in the skin was gone, she cast the child under one of the bushes. Then she went and sat down opposite him a good way off,... for she said, "Do not let me look on the death of the child."... God heard the voice of the boy; and the angel of God called to Hagar..., "What troubles you, Hagar? Do not be afraid; for God has heard the voice of the boy where he is. Come, lift up the boy and hold him fast with your hand, for I will make a great nation of him." Then God opened her eyes and she saw a well of water. She went, and filled the skin with water, and gave the boy a drink.—Genesis 21:9-10,14-19

Anne Hutchinson was a Puritan who immigrated to New England in 1634. She aroused controversy for two reasons: she accused local ministers of preaching a mistaken doctrine, and she provided religious instruction in her home to both men and women. The talks she gave in her home were quite popular with some community members. As a result, she was tried for defamation of the ministers' character, disruption of the peace, and other charges. Following her conviction, she was banished from her community and excommunicated from the church. She moved first to Rhode Island, walking several days through the snow to get there, and then west to a region that is currently part of New York City.

Hutchinson was not as isolated as Hagar, for other communities were willing to accept her. Nor did she have a young child to care for. In providing Abraham a son, Hagar had been obedient to her mistress, yet she was still banished and forced to confront the likelihood of death. Both Anne Hutchinson and Hagar were banished by the very people they relied on for safety and should have been able to trust. The lives of both women remind us of our responsibilities to everyone in our communities, even those who might be troublesome, especially those who are marginalized.

Today's Question

Whom do we cast out or abandon, regardless of the dangers they will be exposed to?

God who creates us,
God who redeems us,

God who sustains us,
help us to remember that your nature
is communal, that as people created in your image,
we live in community.
Teach us to protect rather than endanger,
to listen rather than judge,
to embrace rather than exclude.
May we welcome others as gratefully as we welcome you,
the One who always welcomes us.

Today's Action

Invite a neighbor or a new member of your church out to lunch or over to your house for coffee or tea or take a special treat to a shut-in member of your community.

Anne Hutchinson (1591-1643)

Anne Marbury was born in Lincolnshire, England. She married William Hutchinson in 1612, and they had fifteen children together. They also became acquainted with the Puritan minister John Cotton. He immigrated to Boston, Massachusetts, and the Hutchinsons followed. Anne worked as a midwife and also began hosting religious discussions for women in her home. She aroused controversy, however, when she opened her meetings to men also, for Puritans as well as most other Christians of the time considered it improper for a woman to offer religious instruction to men. Exacerbating this conflict, Anne Hutchinson also began to criticize several local ministers, suggesting that their sermons were based on flawed theology. Debates at that time regarding the nature of faith vs. works were strong, not only in distinguishing between Protestant and Catholic beliefs but also in distinguishing among various Protestant denominations; this debate has become known as the Antinomian Controversy. In 1637, she was tried for heresy, convicted, and banished from the colony. Fortunately, Roger Williams had founded Rhode Island by this time, the only colony at that time that permitted true religious freedom. She moved there and later to the New Netherland's region that is now the Bronx, New York City. She died there in 1643, along with most of her household, when Indians attacked the family.

Day 24

A Samaritan woman came to draw water, and Jesus said to her, "Give me a drink."... The Samaritan woman said to him, "How is it that you, a Jew, ask a drink of me, a woman of Samaria?" (Jews do not share things in common with Samaritans.) Jesus answered her, "If you knew the gift of God, and who it is that is saying to you, 'Give me a drink,' you would have asked him, and he would have given you living water." The woman said to him, "Sir, you have no bucket, and the well is deep. Where do you get that living water?"... Jesus said to her, "Everyone who drinks of this water will be thirsty again, but those who drink of the water that I will give them will never be thirsty. The water that I will give will become in them a spring of water gushing up to eternal life." The woman said to him, "Sir, give me this water ..." Then the woman left her water jar and went back to the city. She said to the people, "Come and see a man who told me everything I have ever done! He cannot be the Messiah, can he?"... Many Samaritans from that city believed in him because of the woman's testimony ... —John 4:7, 9-15, 28-30, 39

Mother Jones was once called "the most dangerous woman in America." Her full name was Mary Harris

Jones, and she suffered significant tragedy in her life. Her husband and four young children died of yellow fever in 1867, and then four years later, she lost her home and business in the Great Chicago Fire. Rather than permit such devastation to defeat her, Mary Harris Jones invested her energy in the nascent labor movement, working as a union organizer. She is perhaps most well known for her Children's Crusade in 1903, a march from Pennsylvania to President Theodore Roosevelt's home in New York in order to protest child labor practices. Legend suggests that thousands of laborers would join a strike at her merest gesture.

We don't often think of the Samaritan woman at the well as particularly dangerous, but many people considered her life scandalous. And for Jesus, a male Jew, to speak publicly to a Samaritan woman was also so unusual that it bordered on scandalous. This encounter, however, prompted her to proclaim the Good News to other Samaritans. Both she and Mother Jones stepped outside of their expected roles in order to speak the truth. Both women led hundreds of others into greater freedom.

Today's Question

How might we use our own voices and tell our own stories in order to liberate others?

God our liberator,
we are grateful for the fresh water

that revives our bodies
and the living water
that enlivens our spirits.
Assist us in our labor,
whether that takes us to the marketplace
in the heat of the day
or the factory floor
in the chill of night.
And when our work is completed,
give us the courage
to proclaim the truth.

Today's Action

Be mindful of water you use throughout the day, as you take a long cool drink or sip warm tea, as you water your plants or garden, or as you take a luxurious bath.

Mary Harris (Mother) Jones (1837-1930)

Mary Harris Jones was born in County Cork, Ireland. Her family immigrated to Canada due to the Irish Potato Famine, and Mary moved to the United States at the age of twenty-three, living in Michigan, Illinois, and Tennessee. She married George E. Jones in Memphis in 1861. George Jones was involved in labor unions. Six years later, George and all four of their children died due to a yellow fever epidemic that swept through Memphis. Mary returned to Chicago, only to see her home and dressmaking business destroyed in the Great Chicago Fire in 1871. Subsequently, she became an activist and union organizer. Her activities frequently pitted her against Catholic priests and bishops who often discouraged labor strikes, and she began to identify herself as agnostic. She assumed the persona of "mother" to the laborers she referred to as her "boys"; she is known today as Mother Jones, with few people knowing her actual name. In 1903, she organized a children's crusade, during which children who had been working in mines and mills marched from Philadelphia to the home of President Theodore Roosevelt in Oyster Bay, New York. She describes her experiences in her autobiography, published in 1925. Her goal was to establish child labor laws as well as laws designed to improve workers' safety. She continued working with unions nearly until her death. Though she died in Maryland, she is buried in the Union Miners Cemetery in Mount Olive, Illinois. The miners themselves raised the money for a substantial gravestone.

Day 25

As [Jacob] looked, he saw a well in the field and three flocks of sheep lying there beside it, for out of that well the flocks were watered. The stone on the well's mouth was large, and when all the flocks were gathered there, the shepherds would roll the stone from the mouth of the well, and water the sheep, and put the stone back in its place on the mouth of the well.... Rachel came with her father's sheep; for she kept them. Now when Jacob saw Rachel, the daughter of his mother's brother Laban, Jacob went up and rolled the stone from the well's mouth, and watered the flock of his mother's brother Laban. Then Jacob kissed Rachel, and wept aloud. And Jacob told Rachel that he was her father's kinsman, and that he was Rebekah's son; and she ran and told her father.—Genesis 29:2-3,9-12

Jane Goodall is best known for her work with chimpanzees in the East African nation of Tanzania. She spent many years studying their behavior, particularly their social interactions. Her methods were unconventional for her time, especially her reception into a chimpanzee group as a virtual member of their tribe. She named the chimpanzees she encountered, describing their distinct personalities rather than simply referring to them by number and claiming scientific objectivity. She challenged the understanding about animals by insisting that chimpanzees expressed affection for one another and also used tools. More recently, Goodall has been an activist for environmentalism and animal protection.

Like Rachel, the keeper of sheep, Goodall interacted with animals much more intimately than many of us in the twenty-first-century developed world do. Rachel would eventually marry Jacob and become mother of two of his sons, and she continues to be rightfully celebrated as an ancestor of Israel. Yet we can also honor her for her expertise as a shepherd, just as we honor Jane Goodall for the good work she has done with chimpanzees. Perhaps you've forgotten some of your own accomplishments, just as the Christian tradition has largely forgotten Rachel's identity as a shepherd. If you are known for one dominant trait or skill, consider the other aspects of your personality and the other ways you have helped to improve the world.

Today's Question

How can you learn to honor your accomplishments?

God who created us
to live among other creatures,
to value and protect them,
help us to remember
our connections to all of creation.

We are grateful
for every talent you've given us.
In valuing them, we honor you.

Today's Action

Visit an animal shelter and volunteer to help walk dogs, socialize cats, or feed and water any of the animals.

Jane Goodall (1934–)

Jane Goodall was born in London, England. She is known for her work with primates, particularly chimpanzees, and she traces her interests to a toy she received as a child, a stuffed chimpanzee she named Jubilee. As a young woman, she traveled to Africa, where she met Richard Leakey, who initially sponsored her work with chimpanzees. She has spent decades studying how they interact socially and within families. Their behavior convinced her that chimps experience emotions, including joy, sorrow, and affection. She concluded that chimpanzees share much with human beings, much more than had been previously thought. She also observed chimps using natural objects as tools, challenging another characteristic that some anthropologists had believed set humans apart from other animals. She noticed a proclivity for violence among both male and female chimps as they sought to establish dominance over other species and within their own troops. To support research on chimpanzees, Goodall established the Jane Goodall Institute in 1977. She has also worked for animal rights and environmental protection and conservation. For both this and her more scientific work, she has won numerous awards, including from the United Nations and from numerous individual countries such as England, France, and Japan. She has written more than two dozen books for adults and children. Although she is not formally affiliated with any religion, she does describe herself as spiritual, experiencing the sacred in nature. She cannot be said to have an actual home, as she travels nearly all year, seldom remaining in one place for more than two or three days at a time.

Day 26

The king of Egypt said to the Hebrew midwives, one of whom was named Shiphrah and the other Puah, "When you act as midwives to the Hebrew women, and see them on the birthstool, if it is a boy, kill him; but if it is a girl, she shall live." But the midwives feared God; they did not do as the king of Egypt commanded them, but they let the boys live. So the king of Egypt summoned the midwives and said to them, "Why have you done this, and allowed the boys to live?" The midwives said to Pharaoh, "Because the Hebrew women are not like the Egyptian women; for they are vigorous and give birth before the midwife comes to them." So God dealt well with the midwives; and the people multiplied and became very strong. And because the midwives feared God, he gave them families.—Exodus 1:15-21

Elizabeth Blackwell was the first woman to earn a Doctor of Medicine degree in the United States. When she initially decided to pursue a medical degree, she met significant opposition. She was finally accepted into the Geneva Medical College in upstate New York due to a prank; the faculty of the college permitted the male students to vote on whether they would permit the admission of a female classmate, and many voted *yes* as a joke. Nevertheless, Blackwell pursued her goal and graduated in 1849. She subsequently studied to be a midwife. With her sister and another physician, she established the New York Infirmary for Women and Children in lower Manhattan in 1857, where additional female doctors received training and poor patients received treatment.

The Egyptian midwives did not challenge professional gender roles, for midwifery was a female task. Yet they did challenge authority, the king's authority no less, because they realized that he was using his authority unjustly and abusing his power. Regardless of who ordered them to, they would not kill children, and they took advantage of the king's ignorance of childbirth to outwit him. Like the midwives of Egypt, Dr. Blackwell resisted the authorities of her day, determined instead to use her intelligence and education for the benefit of the powerless.

Today's Question

What gifts do you have that you could use for the benefit of others?

God our healer,
we know you rejoice with us
as we celebrate each new birth.
We thank you
for the vigor of our bodies,

for the strength of our spirits,
and for the lives of those whose devotion
restores us to health.
Help us to resist those
who urge us toward death,
and keep us ever mindful of the ones
who require our care.

Today's Action

Write a thank-you note to a doctor, nurse, or other health-care worker who has helped you or a member of your family during an illness.

Elizabeth Blackwell (1821-1910)

Elizabeth Blackwell was born into a large family in Bristol, England. The family immigrated to the United States when Elizabeth was eleven years old. Living first in New York City, they eventually settled in Cincinnati, Ohio. During her young adulthood, she taught school in Ohio and Kentucky, though she struggled as a teacher due to some of her religious opinions and because of her discomfort seeing slavery up close in Kentucky. Her father was a Congregationalist Christian, but Elizabeth converted briefly to Episcopalianism and then to Unitarianism after being introduced to the ideas of Transcendentalism. During this time, she decided to pursue a medical education but was not taken seriously by several of the schools she applied to. They sometimes offered her the contradictory response that women were intellectually inferior to men, but that they weren't willing to take the chance that a woman could exceed the performance of the men in their studies. Eventually, Geneva Medical College in Geneva, New York, accepted her application after the male students agreed that she should be admitted. She received her medical degree on January 23, 1849, the first woman in the United States to do so. She continued her medical education in Europe. When she returned to the United States, she attempted to practice medicine but could attract few patients. With her sister Emily, who had also become a doctor, and Marie Zakrzewska, another woman physician, Blackwell established the New York Infirmary for Indigent Women and Children. During her time as a physician, she wrote several books focusing on the role of women in medicine. She eventually returned to England and died in the city of Hastings in 1910.

Day 27

> There was also a prophet, Anna the daughter of Phanuel, of the tribe of Asher. She was of a great age, having lived with her husband seven years after her marriage, then as a widow to the age of eighty-four. She never left the temple but worshiped there with fasting and prayer night and day. At that moment she came, and began to praise God and to speak about the child to all who were looking for the redemption of Jerusalem.—Luke 2:36-38

During the Late Middle Ages, Julian of Norwich lived in isolation in a room in the local churchyard in order to devote herself to prayer, although people visited her for spiritual guidance. During a severe illness, Julian experienced a series of visions during which Christ appeared to her and spoke with her. After she recovered, she described the visions in her *Revelations of Divine Love,* generally considered the earliest book written in English by a woman. Like many other mystics, Julian experienced God as a loving Creator and Savior, and she referred to God as both mother and father. These visions led her to her most famous statement, one of the most optimistic theological insights in all of Christianity: "It behoved that there should be sin; but all shall be well, and all shall be well, and all manner of things shall be well."

We often think of prophets as those who can predict the future, but biblical prophets are more accurately described as those who perceive God's will and are inspired to speak it. Anna was a prophet because she immediately recognized the identity of Jesus, which she was able to do because she spent so much of her life in prayer. Her spiritual disciplines prepared her for that moment when she saw the infant Jesus. Despite their differences in time and place, Julian's life was remarkably similar to Anna's, for she too devoted herself to prayer and other spiritual practices. Both Anna and Julian are celebrated for their new ways of recognizing the Divine.

Today's Question

If you were to encounter God in a divine vision, how would you respond?

God our visionary,
we know that you reveal yourself
in the ordinary and the extraordinary.
When we become complacent,
startle us into awareness;
when we ask for a sign,
remind us to look toward creation.
Yet we continue to ask
for complete unity with you,

and for knowledge of your presence
in our minds, our souls, our hearts, and our bodies.
Even when we fail to recognize your presence,
we ask for your assurance
that all is well
and all shall be well.

Today's Action

Write in your journal about the aspects of your life that help you believe "all shall be well."

Julian of Norwich (c. 1342–c. 1416)

Julian of Norwich was a medieval English mystic and author of *Revelations of Divine Love,* which describes her mystical experiences. Little is known about her early life, though scholars believe it is likely that she was from Norwich, England, or a nearby town. Her family might have been wealthy. She became an anchorite; that is, she lived alone in a cell attached to St. Julian's church in Norwich. Some historians believe she was a nun, but there is no definitive evidence of that. Her era was marked by epidemics of the plague and other events that seemed to indicate the world was unreliable. She herself suffered a serious illness when she was thirty years old, and when a priest, believing she was near death, held a crucifix above her bed, she had several visions of Jesus. By the time the visions concluded, she was healed. She described these visions in her *Revelations*, continuing to revise it for several years as she explored the theological meaning of the visions. It is here that she wrote her best-known words, "All shall be well." Her book is believed to be the oldest one written by a woman in English. A shrine to her currently stands on the site of her cell, and the city of Norwich currently hosts an annual weeklong festival in her honor.

Day 28

Mordecai told them to reply to Esther, "Do not think that in the king's palace you will escape any more than all the other Jews. For if you keep silence at such a time as this, relief and deliverance will rise for the Jews from another quarter, but you and your father's family will perish. Who knows? Perhaps you have come to royal dignity for just such a time as this." Then Esther said in reply to Mordecai, "Go, gather all the Jews to be found in Susa, and hold a fast on my behalf, and neither eat nor drink for three days, night or day. I and my maids will also fast as you do. After that I will go to the king, though it is against the law; and if I perish, I perish." Mordecai then went away and did everything as Esther had ordered him.—Esther 4:13-16

Emma Lazarus was a poet and author who embraced her Jewish ancestry as she learned about the Russian pogroms and the plight of Jewish immigrants seeking refuge in the United States. She was a renowned poet and the author of "The New Colossus," the poem engraved on a bronze plaque in the pedestal of the Statue of Liberty. Many of us are familiar with the lines: "Give me your tired, your poor, / Your huddled masses yearning to breathe free." The poem acknowledges that many immigrants arrive in America because of desperate circumstances in their home countries. But the poem also honors the statue itself with these earlier lines: "Here at our sea-washed, sunset gates shall stand / A mighty woman with a torch, whose flame / Is the imprisoned lightning, and her name / Mother of Exiles."

Though she was married to the Persian king, Queen Esther was an exile. She was Jewish, though her husband was unaware of that fact. She realized, however, that hiding who she was would not save her. Following a plot to kill numerous Jews, Esther risked her own life, revealed her identity, and saved her people. Emma Lazarus herself was born in the United States and so not an exile like Queen Esther. In fact, her family had immigrated to the American continent centuries before and was well connected. She was writing, however, as anti-Semitic violence was increasing in Russia, and many Russian Jews were immigrating to the United States. In both situations, Jews were persecuted simply for being who they were. Like Esther, Emma Lazarus used the power of her voice to save others.

Today's Question

When have you spoken up to support the powerless?

God who spoke the world into being,
remind me that I too can speak,
that I can speak out and speak up.

And when I speak, give me the wisdom
to discern what to say.
Remind me that I too am a mighty woman
whose words can bring others
into freedom.

Today's Action

Get involved in a local anti-bullying program, one that seeks to protect people from harassment and violence that has become so common in our culture. You might consider an organization that works to protect children or elderly people, survivors of domestic violence, LGBTQ people, or individuals living with mental illnesses or addictions.

Emma Lazarus (1849-1887)

Emma Lazarus was born in and lived her entire life (except for two long trips to Europe) in New York City. She was Jewish, and her family had lived in New York for many generations. She did not attend public school; rather, her family hired private tutors to provide her education. Lazarus was a well-known author who wrote poetry, a novel, and two plays. In part because of her own fame, she was acquainted with many other significant literary and artistic figures, including Ralph Waldo Emerson and William Morris. She is best known today for her poem "The New Colossus," which is inscribed on a plaque in the base of the Statue of Liberty. She wrote the poem as part of a fundraising project for the statue's pedestal, which needed to be built before the statue could be placed in New York Harbor. Lazarus also wrote articles addressing the history of discrimination against Jewish people, especially in Russia, and she helped organize vocational education for newly arrived Jewish immigrants. She supported the establishment of a Jewish state long before the re-establishment of Israel became a reality in 1948. She returned home seriously ill from her second European trip and died a few weeks later.

Day 29

> [Jesus] said, "In a certain city there was a judge who neither feared God nor had respect for the people. In that city there was a widow who kept coming to him and saying, 'Grant me justice against my opponent.' For a while he refused; but later he said to himself, 'Though I have no fear of God and no respect for anyone, yet because this widow keeps bothering me, I will grant her justice, so that she may not wear me out by continually coming.'" And the Lord said, "Listen to what the unjust judge says. And will not God grant justice to his chosen ones who cry to him day and night? Will he delay long in helping them? I tell you, he will quickly grant justice to them."—Luke 18:2-8a

Sojourner Truth was born towards the end of the eighteenth century. In 1843, after embracing Christianity, she changed her name from Isabella Baumfree to Sojourner Truth because she had walked many miles to teach and preach the truth of the gospel and to argue for women's rights and the abolition of slavery. It's been said that because of her size and build, someone once accused her of being a man. So she bared her breasts and proclaimed her famous speech, often called "Ain't I a Woman."

In her autobiography, she tells a story involving, if not a judge as in the passage above, at least a grand jury. Sojourner Truth was enslaved in New York just as slavery was becoming illegal there. The new law stated that no slaves could be sold out of state—so that masters hoping to recoup their wealth couldn't sell their soon-to-be-emancipated slaves in the remaining slave states. One of Truth's masters had sold her son, Peter, in violation of this law. Truth went to the courthouse, swore that her son was in fact her son, and obtained a writ directing that Peter be returned to her. She succeeded through the assistance of several others and through her own persistence. Although her path to justice wasn't always clear to her, her way became clear as she refused to give up or give in. Like the persistent widow in the story from Luke, Sojourner Truth was convinced of the righteousness of her case. The widow's judge ironically seems indifferent to justice, but he nevertheless responds. The widow heard the word "no," but decided to interpret it as "not yet," refusing to let the judge get away with ignoring her. Perhaps you've had a similar experience, achieving justice because you refused to give up.

Today's Question

What influences you to persist in your quest for justice?

God my liberator,
I ask that you help me see the way
to truth and justice clearly.

I ask that you restore my determination
when my hope wanes.
And I ask that when I am called to judge,
I do so with fairness and respect.

Today's Action

Pray for those who daily bear the responsibility of making, enforcing, and interpreting the law, that their decisions will be fair and wise.

Sojourner Truth (c. 1797–1883)

Sojourner Truth was born as an enslaved person in Ulster County, New York, and named Isabella Baumfree. During her childhood, she was sold to multiple different owners. While she was a child, New York began a complicated process of gradual emancipation. Adults would be emancipated first, and children would be emancipated when they reached adulthood, until emancipation was complete. A clause in the law forbade slave owners from selling their enslaved people out of state in order to recoup their investments. Nevertheless, one of Truth's sons, Peter, was sold to a slaveholder in Alabama. She went to court to sue the owner for his freedom, a case she won in a rare instance of an African American woman prevailing legally over a white man prior to the Civil War. During this period, Truth became a devout Christian. She changed her name to Sojourner Truth, citing that she walked from place to place offering testimony about her religious experience and arguing for abolition and women's rights, and that she always spoke the truth. Her memoir, *The Narrative of Sojourner Truth,* was published in 1850. A year later, she made her most famous speech, "Ain't I a Woman," when a man challenged her to prove that she was a woman because of her size. During the Civil War, she continued her work by assisting Union soldiers and newly freed people. She died in Battle Creek, Michigan, where she had been living for several years, and is buried there in Oak Hill Cemetery.

Day 30

Naomi said to her two daughters-in-law, "Go back each of you to your mother's house. May the LORD deal kindly with you as you have dealt with the dead and with me. The LORD grant that you may find security, each of you in the house of your husband." Then she kissed them and they wept aloud.... Naomi her mother-in-law said to [Ruth], "My daughter, I need to seek some security for you, so that it may be well with you."... So Boaz took Ruth and she became his wife. When they came together, the LORD made her conceive, and she bore a son.... Then Naomi took the child and laid him in her bosom, and became his nurse.—Ruth 1:8-9; 3:1; 4:13,16

Jane Addams was active in many causes but is most closely associated with Hull House, which she cofounded with Ellen Gates Starr in 1889. Hull House was one of the first settlement houses where individuals from different social classes and ethnic backgrounds lived in community, practicing democratic and egalitarian ideals. Hull House was staffed primarily by women who were invested in increased professional opportunities for women. The modern profession of social work owes much of its success to Jane Addams, and many of the early residents of Hull House became prominent social reformers later in their lives. Through the work of Addams and her colleagues, settlement houses provided a means toward assimilation for new American immigrants.

Naomi was concerned with the welfare of both her daughters-in-law, and Ruth remains known today for her reciprocal care for Naomi. They were concerned for each other's physical and emotional survival, for their security within cultures that did not prioritize the security of women. Like Naomi cared for her daughter-in-law, Jane Addams created a space where others could feel secure. You might also have experienced a time when you worried for your own security. When we feel secure ourselves, we are called to create that security for others.

Today's Question

Who has looked out for you and contributed to your security?

God our security,
we too often surrender
to anxiety, worried
about tomorrow and the next day.
Our futures often feel uncertain,
and our world unpredictable.
When we fear
there is no one to depend on,
recall us to our faith

in you, our reliance
on you, God of our ancestors
and our descendants,
God who was and is
and always will be.

Today's Action

Bring something special to someone whose future is uncertain—a bouquet of flowers, a scented candle, a piece of pottery, or something else that will assure her she is cared for.

Jane Addams (1860-1935)

Born in Cedarville, Illinois, Jane Addams came from a politically engaged family, which probably influenced her later contributions to the social welfare of many people, particularly women, immigrants, and children in Chicago. As a young woman, she attended Rockford Female Seminary and subsequently completed one year at the Women's Medical College of Philadelphia. A few years later, after reading about settlement houses, she arranged to visit the original one, Toynbee Hall in London. She was attracted to the concept, which not only provided practical assistance to people in need but also facilitated interactions among people of different social and ethnic backgrounds. Returning to the United States, she cofounded Hull House with her friend Ellen Gates Starr in 1889. The building, a mansion previously owned by Charles Hull, eventually provided living space for about two dozen women, as well as meeting space for adult education, music instruction, drama productions, and other activities. Her religious practices varied over the course of her life. Baptized a Presbyterian, she maintained her membership in that denomination, but she also attended a Unitarian church in Chicago and established close connections with members of a Jewish congregation. Considered the founder of social work in the United States, she supported many progressive causes, including women's rights, pacifism, and prohibition. She published many articles and books, including her memoir, *Twenty Years at Hull House,* in 1910. In 1931, she won the Nobel Peace Prize, the first American woman to be so honored. She died in Chicago at the age of seventy-four and is buried in Cedarville, Illinois.

Day 31

Now while Jesus was at Bethany in the house of Simon the leper, a woman came to him with an alabaster jar of very costly ointment, and she poured it on his head as he sat at the table. But when the disciples saw it, they were angry and said, "Why this waste? For this ointment could have been sold for a large sum, and the money given to the poor." But Jesus, aware of this, said to them, "Why do you trouble the woman? She has performed a good service for me. For you always have the poor with you, but you will not always have me. By pouring this ointment on my body she has prepared me for burial. Truly I tell you, wherever this good news is proclaimed in the whole world, what she has done will be told in remembrance of her."—Matthew 26:6-13

Maya Lin is the architect who designed the Vietnam Veterans Memorial in Washington, DC. Her design was initially controversial, for some people believed it lacked the heroic grandeur we often attribute to war memorials, but it has become one of the most visited sites in the country. Composed of reflective black granite engraved with the names of more than fifty thousand soldiers who died during the conflict, the monument is emotionally moving because the names individualize the men and women honored and remembered there. Visitors can touch the names of their sons, brothers, fathers, and friends, as a tangible sign of their memory. Although Lin was only twenty-one years old when she submitted her design, she seems to have understood what other Americans needed to help them heal from this war. If you've visited the monument, you understand how it honors the lives of those who died and the grief of those who survived.

In this story from Matthew's Gospel, Jesus understood that the time of his death was approaching. The woman who anointed him might not have known why he was suffering at that moment, but she understood what he needed, and she offered it to him. Many of us—perhaps you as well—find ourselves in situations in which our need for spiritual healing exceeds practical considerations. Sometimes the very action that makes us most vulnerable is most healing.

Today's Question

What is it in you that most needs healing?

God of memory,
recall our names as you heal the wounds
we expose to you.
Remind us of the names,
one by one by one,

of people whose lives ended in violence.
In their memory, may we work
toward a world
of safety and wholeness,
each of us anointed
and anointing.

Today's Action

Write down the names of people you know who need healing. Pray for them, one by one, and let your prayers lead you to offer what they need.

Maya Lin (1959-)

Maya Lin was born in Athens, Ohio. Her parents were immigrants from China who taught at Ohio University. Always interested in art, Lin attended Yale University, earning a BA in 1981 and a Masters of Architecture in 1986. When she was still an undergraduate, she achieved sudden fame when she won a competition to design the Vietnam Veterans Memorial; nearly fifteen hundred entries had been submitted. Because it does not feature the traditional heroic sculpture celebrating war, Lin's design was initially controversial. The memorial is a seemingly endless wall that lists the names of all the soldiers who died or remain missing. Soon after it was built in 1982, it became one of the most visited places in

Washington, DC. In this and other work, Lin is interested in how human creations interact with the environment. In the years since she designed the Vietnam Veterans Memorial, she has designed numerous large-scale pieces of architecture and earthworks, including the Civil Rights Memorial in Montgomery, Alabama, and the Museum of Chinese in America in New York City. She has received several prestigious awards, including the Presidential Medal of Freedom, and her work is displayed in sites as varied as Pennsylvania Station in New York City; the Cleveland Public Library in Cleveland, Ohio; and the Langston Hughes Library in Clinton, Tennessee. She is married to photographer Daniel Wolf, and they have two daughters. She currently lives in New York City.

Timeline of Featured Women

c. 1342–c. 1416	Julian of Norwich, English, mystic, and writer.
1591–1643	Anne Hutchinson, English and American, religious leader.
1600–1672	Elizabeth Hooton, English, evangelist.
1614–1702	Margaret Fell Fox, English, evangelist.
c. 1797–1883	Sojourner Truth, African American, evangelist, women's rights activist.
1819–1910	Julia Ward Howe, American, writer.
1821–1910	Elizabeth Blackwell, English and American, doctor.
c. 1822–1913	Harriet Tubman, African American, escaped slave, conductor on the Underground Railroad.
1837–1930	Mary Harris Jones (Mother Jones), Irish and American, labor activist.
1849–1887	Emma Lazarus, American, writer.
1856–1944	Pretty Shield, Native American (Crow), medicine woman.
1860–1935	Jane Addams, American, social worker.

1867–1932 Margaret Tobin (Molly) Brown, American, philanthropist.

1891–1960 Zora Neale Hurston, African American, writer, anthropologist.

1897–1980 Dorothy Day, American, journalist, social reformer.

1908–1981 Mildred Norman Ryder (Peace Pilgrim), American, peace activist.

1920–1951 Henrietta Lacks, African American, mother, cancer patient.

1925–; 1935– Stefania and Helena Podgórska, Polish and American, Righteous Gentiles of the Holocaust.

1934– Jane Goodall, English, primatologist.

1940–2012 Rebecca Brown, American, activist with Mothers Against Drunk Driving.

1940– Maxine Hong Kingston, Chinese American, writer.

1942– Verna Fowler, Native American (Menominee), religious sister, educator.

1943 Rosie the Riveter, American, fictional character, cultural icon.

1944– Alice Waters, American, chef, author, activist.

1947– Temple Grandin, American, animal scientist, autism activist.

1954–	Ruby Bridges, African American, civil-rights activist.
1954–	Sonia Sotomayor, American, Supreme Court justice.
1959–	Maya Lin, Chinese American, architect.
1972–	Angela Warnick Buchdahl, Korean American, rabbi.
1985–2012	Victoria Leigh Soto, American, teacher.
1987–	Elizabeth Smart, American, kidnap victim, children's rights activist.

For Further Reading

Many of the books that are by the women featured in these devotions are mentioned in their biographies and do not appear below. Listed here are books focused on additional significant women.

Castor, Helen. *Joan of Arc: A History.* Harper Perennial, 2016.

Comfort, Ray and Trish Ramos. *Susanna Wesley: Her Remarkable Life.* Bridge-Logos Publishers, 2014.

Epstein, Daniel Mark. *Sister Aimee: The Life of Aimee Semple McPherson.* Mariner Books, 2014.

Francis, Richard. *Ann the Word: The Story of Ann Lee, Female Messiah, Mother of the Shakers, the Woman Clothed with the Sun.* Penguin Books, 2001.

Gillian, Gill. *Mary Baker Eddy.* Da Capo Press, 1999.

Green, Roger Joseph. *Catherine Booth: A Biography of the Cofounder of the Salvation Army.* Baker Publishing Group, 1996.

Lee, Jarena. *Religious Experience and Journal of Mrs. Jarena Lee, Giving an Account of Her Call to Preach the Gospel.* In *Spiritual Narratives.* Oxford University Press, 1991.

Lindbergh, Anne Morrow. *A Gift from the Sea.* Pantheon, 1991.

Merwin, Anne. *Elizabeth Ann Seton.* Paulist Books, 2015.

Miles, Sara. *Take This Bread: A Radical Conversion.* Ballantine Books, 2008.

Plimpton, Ruth Talbot. *Mary Dyer: Biography of a Rebel Quaker.* Brandon Books, 2009.

Spink, Kathryn. *Mother Teresa: An Authorized Biography.* HarperCollins, 2011.

Thiel, Mark G. and Christopher Vesey. *Native Footsteps: Along the Path of Saint Kateri Tekakwitha.* Marquette University Press, 2013.